Boots

COOKSHOP

MEDITERRANEAN COOKERY

Boots

COOKSHOP

MEDITERRANEAN COOKERY

Front cover photograph by Dave Jordan
shows Valencian Paella (page 52)

Published 1986 on behalf of
The Boots Company Plc Nottingham England
by Hamlyn Publishing
Bridge House, London Road, Twickenham, Middlesex,
England

ISBN 0 600 32653 5

Set in 10/11pt Gill Sans Light
by Photocomp Ltd, Birmingham

Printed in Italy

Contents

Useful Facts & Figures

Notes on metrication

In this book quantities are given in metric and Imperial measures. Exact conversion from Imperial to metric measures does not usually give very convenient working quantities and so the metric measures have been rounded off into units of 25 grams. The table below shows the recommended equivalents.

Ounces	Approx g to nearest whole figure	Recommended conversion to nearest unit of 25
1	28	25
2	57	50
3	85	75
4	113	100
5	142	150
6	170	175
7	198	200
8	227	225
9	255	250
10	283	275
11	312	300
12	340	350
13	368	375
14	396	400
15	425	425
16 (1 lb)	454	450
17	482	475
18	510	500
19	539	550
20 (1¼ lb)	567	575

Note: When converting quantities over 20 oz first add the appropriate figures in the centre column, then adjust to the nearest unit of 25. As a general guide, 1 kg (1000 g) equals 2·2 lb or about 2 lb 3 oz. This method of conversion gives good results in nearly all cases, although in certain pastry and cake recipes a more accurate conversion is necessary to produce a balanced recipe.

Liquid measures The millilitre has been used in this book and the following table gives a few examples.

Imperial	Approx ml to nearest whole figure	Recommended ml
¼ pint	142	150 ml
½ pint	283	300 ml
¾ pint	425	450 ml
1 pint	567	600 ml
1½ pints	851	900 ml
1¾ pints	992	1000 ml (1 litre)

Spoon measures All spoon measures given in this book are level unless otherwise stated.

Can sizes At present, cans are marked with the exact (usually to the nearest whole number) metric equivalent of the Imperial weight of the contents, so we have followed this practice when giving can sizes.

Oven temperatures

The table below gives recommended equivalents.

	°C	°F	Gas
Very cool	110	225	¼
	120	250	½
Cool	140	275	1
	150	300	2
Moderate	160	325	3
	180	350	4
Moderately hot	190	375	5
	200	400	6
Hot	220	425	7
	230	450	8
Very hot	240	475	9

Note: *When making any of the recipes in this book, only follow one set of measures as they are not interchangeable.*

Fish Soup with Lemon Sauce (page 21)

Introduction

The cuisine of the Mediterranean countries must be among the most colourful in the world. Rich in the use of olive oil or dairy foods, enlivened with garlic or zesty lemons and fragrant with fresh herbs, mouth-watering dishes of seafood, poultry, meat, vegetables, rice and pasta are prepared daily in the most humble of homes. The whole subject of food, cooking and eating forms an important part of everyday life. Fast foods and convenience packages have no place here where many hours a day may be spent selecting the perfect ingredients, preparing the food, marinating the meats and cooking the meal to perfection. The emphasis is on good, flavoursome and satisfying cooking; wholesome family meals, served with local wines and fresh bread are just as important to the cook as great feasts or celebrations.

The variety of Mediterranean ingredients which have over many centuries been used to create the aromatic dishes of these countries are now widely available in most supermarkets – aubergines, okra, garlic, fine onions, shiny peppers and a variety of tomatoes can be purchased along with rice, pulses, cheese of all types, pasta and other specialist items. The following brief glossary lists some unusual ingredients you will find in the recipes.

Beetroot Leaves Beetroot is usually sold stripped of its leaves but if you grow your own then the leaves can be used in cooking. Spinach can be substituted.

Borage A small herb with bright blue flowers. It is used to flavour drinks as well as in cooking. The tender young leaves are also used in salads. Dried borage can be used.

Broad Beans, dried When dried, broad beans are wrinkled and brown. Available from health food shops.

Brown Beans Small dried brown beans, also known as ful medames. Available from health food shops.

Capers Small, dark green, unopened buds of a shrub, sold pickled in vinegar. They are piquant with a peppery taste and are used in small quantities to flavour fish, poultry and meat dishes or sauces. They are also employed as a garnish.

Chick Peas Small pulses about the size of dried peas. Require lengthy soaking before cooking. Served whole or ground, hot or cold. Also available canned.

Chick Pea Flour A fine flour made from ground chick peas. Available from ethnic shops and health food shops.

Cotechino Sausage A spicy, Italian pork sausage which is available part-cured like a salami from delicatessens. It is cooked before serving.

Cumin Small elongated seeds (usually white but black are also used in Indian cooking). Available ground from supermarkets also available whole from health food shops and ethnic shops.

Okra Also known as Lady's Fingers, ridged green pods which vary in size. Commonly available fresh, the ends are trimmed off before cooking and the pods washed.

Olive Oil Olive trees are a feature of the countryside all over the Mediterranean. The trees yield olives which are then pickled or from which olive oil is extracted. It is used extensively in Mediterranean cooking, and often in large quantities. Its distinct qualities gives dishes their essential characteristic flavour.

Available from all supermarkets, delicatessens and health food shops, there are many different grades of olive oil. The prime, virgin oil is taken from the best fresh olives which are crushed to extract it. This oil will have a strong taste and smell and a dark green colour. The fruit can be crushed a second time to extract an inferior oil which has a weaker flavour and less pronounced colour.

The virgin oils, the ones with the fullest flavour and deepest colour, are usually available from Italian delicatessens and occasionally from good supermarkets. Lighter oils with a weaker flavour are to be found in most supermarkets. If you do intend to use olive oil frequently, then find a good delicatessen which sells cans of the oil and it will be significantly cheaper.

Orange-flower Water Water scented with the flowers of orange trees. Use as a flavouring for sweets.

Parmesan Cheese A hard, strongly flavoured Italian cheese which is commonly available. Best used freshly grated. The grated cheese can be frozen and used straight from the freezer.

Pecorino Cheese An Italian hard cheese made from sheep's milk. Available from delicatessens. Parmesan can be substituted.

Phylo Pastry Very thin sheets of fine pastry available fresh or frozen from delicatessens. The pastry is brushed with melted butter before cooking. Keep the pastry covered with cling film to prevent it drying out.

Pine-nut Kernels Small oval, pale-coloured kernels of the pine tree. They have a delicate flavour and are used in both savoury and sweet recipes. Available from good supermarkets, delicatessens and health food shops.

Ricotta Cheese A soft unsalted cream cheese from Italy. Available in good supermarkets, delicatessens or Italian shops.

Rosewater Water scented with rose leaves. Available from chemists and health food shops. Used to flavour sweetmeats and desserts.

Serrano Ham Sweet cured ham from Spain, usually eaten raw. Available from delicatessens. Prosciutto can be used instead.

Tahina Also known as tahini. This is a pale, creamy paste made from ground sesame seeds. Available from health food shops and delicatessens.

Vine Leaves Available canned or vacuum packed from good supermarkets and delicatessens. Rinse well. Usually stuffed with rice or meat.

Pizza Margherita (page 40)

Egypt

Egyptian civilisation dates back many thousands of years, and many different rulers have come and gone, leaving their varied influences on the country's culture and cuisine. The strongest and most lasting of these was that of the Ottoman Turks, and most Egyptian dishes are similar to those found in Istanbul, though a few traditional ones do remain, some peculiar to south and upper Egypt and others more Alexandrian in origin. However, some Egyptian dishes, although they have their equivalents elsewhere in the Eastern Mediterranean, have acquired their own national character, the way they are prepared being wholly Egyptian, and these are the ones found on the following pages.

BAKED FISH

SERVES 4

Any type of fish between 7·5 and 30 cm/3 and 12 in long may be used for this recipe.

4 mackerel or trout
salt and pepper
8 medium tomatoes
4 large onions
1 tablespoon chopped fresh basil or
2 teaspoons dried basil
3 tablespoons olive oil

Clean the fish and remove and discard the heads. Place the opened underside of each fish on a board and press firmly along the backbone to loosen the flesh from the bone. Turn the fish over and ease out the backbone. Rinse the fish under cold running water, then dry with a cloth or kitchen paper and sprinkle with salt and pepper. Set the oven at moderate (160 C, 325 F, gas 3).

Drop the tomatoes into boiling water for 1 minute, then peel and thinly slice them. Peel and thinly slice the onions. Place half the onion and tomato slices in the bottom of a roasting tin or ovenproof dish and sprinkle with half the basil. Place the fish on top, cover with the remaining onion and tomato slices, the remaining basil and seasoning to taste. Sprinkle the olive oil over the top and cook in the pre-heated oven for 40 to 45 minutes or until the flesh of the fish is firm and white and the onions are soft.

If necessary, transfer the fish to a heated serving dish, arranging the onions and tomatoes on top. Serve immediately.

CHICKEN WITH LENTILS

SERVES 4 to 6

450 g/1 lb red lentils, presoaked
1 chicken, about 1·4 kg/3 lb
1 large onion
100 g/4 oz butter or margarine
1 tablespoon ground cumin
salt and pepper

Soak the lentils overnight or for at least 2 hours in plenty of cold water, then drain them. Wipe the chicken inside and out with a damp cloth or kitchen paper, and cut it into eight portions. Peel and coarsely chop the onion.

Melt half the butter or margarine in a large, heavy frying pan over a moderate heat and sauté the onion and chicken together until both start to brown. Drain and transfer to a casserole. Add the lentils, cumin, seasoning to taste and just enough water to cover. Dot the remaining butter or margarine over the top, and cook in a moderately hot oven (190 C, 375 F, gas 5) for about 1 hour or until the chicken is tender and most of the liquid has been absorbed. Stir the mixture occasionally while cooking. Serve hot from the casserole.

Chicken Supreme

SERVES 4

This dish is particularly suited to hot climates. Served cold, it is an excellent buffet dish for large parties or for luncheons.

1 chicken, about 1·4 kg/3 lb
2 medium carrots
1 large onion
2-3 celery sticks, about 7·5 cm/3 in long
salt and pepper
50 g/2 oz plain flour
300 ml/½ pint milk
1½ tablespoons lemon juice

Place the chicken in a large saucepan with just enough water to cover. Peel the carrots and the onion and wash the celery sticks under cold running water. Add the carrots, onion, celery and seasoning to taste to the saucepan, place over a moderate heat and bring to the boil. Lower the heat and simmer for 45 to 50 minutes or until the chicken is tender.

Remove the chicken from the stock and set it aside to drain and cool. Boil the chicken stock until reduced to about 600 ml/1 pint and set aside until required. Discard the vegetables.

When the chicken is cool enough to handle, remove the meat from the bones. Cut the meat into large pieces, and arrange it on a serving dish.

Blend the flour in a saucepan with a little of the milk to a smooth, soft paste, then gradually add the remaining milk and the chicken stock. Place the pan over a moderate heat and bring to the boil, stirring constantly until the sauce is smooth and thick. Stir in the lemon juice and adjust the seasoning if necessary.

Stir until just warm, then pour the sauce over the chicken and set aside to cool completely before serving.

Baked Fish (opposite page)

Stuffed Vine Leaves

SERVES 4

1 large onion
25 g/1 oz butter or 2 tablespoons oil
100 g/4 oz long-grain rice
600 ml/1 pint lamb or chicken stock
225 g/8 oz lean minced lamb
1 tablespoon freshly chopped parsley
salt and pepper
2 teaspoons lemon juice
16 vine leaves (from a can or packet)

Peel and chop the onion. Melt the butter or oil in a saucepan. Fry the onion until just soft and transparent, then add the rice. Pour in 300 ml/½ pint of the stock. Bring to the boil, then reduce the heat and simmer gently for about 15 to 20 minutes until the rice is just cooked and the stock has been absorbed.

Remove from the heat, stir in the lamb, parsley, seasoning and lemon juice. Make sure all the ingredients are thoroughly combined. Lay a vine leaf flat on the work surface. Place a spoonful of the mixture in the centre of the leaf. Fold the sides and ends around the filling to make a neat parcel. Place in an ovenproof dish. Fill the remaining leaves in the same way.

Pour the remaining stock over the stuffed vine leaves. Cover and cook in a moderate oven (180C, 375F, gas 4) for 1 hour. Leave to cool or serve warm. Lift the vine leaves out of the cooking liquid with a perforated spoon.

Stuffed Vine Leaves with Calf's Foot

SERVES 6

Stuffed vine leaves are found all over the Mediterranean, but this enriched method of preparing them is traditionally Egyptian, as is the custom of serving them with natural yogurt.

1 calf's foot or foreshank
2 medium onions
3 celery leaves, about 7·5 cm/3 in long
1 sprig fresh dill
2 bay leaves
salt and pepper
Stuffed Vine Leaves (left)
300 ml/½ pint natural yogurt

Wash the calf's foot or foreshank and rinse it well under cold running water. Peel the onions and leave them whole. Place the calf's foot and onions in a large saucepan, add the celery leaves, dill, bay leaves, seasoning to taste and cold water to cover, place over a moderate heat and bring to the boil. Lower the heat and simmer, partially covered, for about 2 hours. Remove the calf's foot from the saucepan and set it aside to cool. Strain and reserve the stock, discarding the onions and herbs.

Prepare and stuff the vine leaves according to the recipe instructions. Place them very close together in a saucepan, arranging them in several layers if necessary. Cover them with the stock and place a small plate over the top layer of leaves. Tightly cover the saucepan and simmer over a low heat for 1 to 1¼ hours. Drain off the stock and arrange the stuffed vine leaves on a plate.

Thinly slice the meat from the calf's foot and sprinkle the slices over the stuffed vine leaves. Serve cold. Serve with the yogurt, offered in a separate dish.

AUBERGINES IN TAHINA SAUCE

SERVES 4

This is a superb way of serving aubergines as a cold dish. Here the Egyptians combine the Lebanese tahina with a Turkish aubergine salad. Tahina (sesame paste) is made from ground sesame seeds and is usually sold in jars. It can be bought in shops specialising in Oriental foods or in most health food shops.

2 large aubergines
few drops lemon juice
salt and pepper
1 teaspoon chopped fresh parsley
Sauce
2 tablespoons tahina
1½ tablespoons lemon juice
salt and pepper
1 teaspoon olive oil

Wash the aubergines and dry them, then place them in a moderately hot oven (200C, 400F, gas 6) for 15 to 20 minutes or until the skins are browned and the aubergines are limp. Remove them from the oven and when they are cool enough to handle, cut them in half lengthways and remove the pulpy flesh, discarding the skins. Mash the flesh in a bowl with a few drops of the lemon juice, seasoning to taste and the parsley.

To make the sauce, mix the *tahina* in a bowl with enough cold water to give a soft, creamy consistency similar to that of mayonnaise. Stir in the lemon juice, a little salt and pepper to taste and the olive oil.

Mix the aubergine pulp into the *tahina* sauce and allow to cool. Garnish with lemon wedges and parsley. Serve cold with warmed pitta bread.

Aubergines in Tahina Sauce

Broad Bean Balls

MAKES ABOUT 24

These broad bean balls are sometimes eaten with the local flat pitta bread and tomatoes or onions. Dried broad beans are available from health food shops.

100 g/4 oz dried broad beans, presoaked
salt and pepper
½ teaspoon chopped fresh parsley
3 tablespoons olive oil
oil for deep-frying

Drain the beans well and remove their skins, then crush the beans into small pieces in a mortar, on a board with a rolling pin, or in a food processor. Place in a saucepan with seasoning to taste and just enough water to cover. Bring to the boil over a moderate heat. Lower the heat, tightly cover the saucepan and simmer for 20 to 30 minutes or until all the liquid has been absorbed. Remove from the heat, stir in the chopped parsley and olive oil. Allow to cool.

With damp hands, roll the mixture into balls and set aside for about 1 hour. Deep-fry in the hot oil until golden brown. Drain on kitchen paper and serve hot or cold with a *Tahina* Dip (below).

Broad Bean Balls with Tahina Dip

Tahina Dip

Stir 150 ml/¼ pint tahina into 150 ml/¼ pint natural yogurt. Add 1 crushed clove garlic, 2 tablespoons lemon juice and seasoning to taste. Chill the dip and serve with the Broad Bean Balls.

Lentil Purée

SERVES 6

Lentils were an important part of the diet of the ancient Egyptians, and were recorded in the provision lists found by archeologists in the Old Kingdom temples. They are still extensively used today.

2 large onions
450 g/1 lb red lentils
1 tablespoon ground cumin
salt and pepper
4 tablespoons olive oil

Peel and slice one of the onions, place it in a saucepan with the lentils and add enough water to cover. Bring to the boil over a moderate heat, lower the heat, tightly cover the pan and simmer for 20 to 30 minutes or until the lentils become soft and pulpy. Drain off any excess water and purée in a liquidiser or food processor. Stir in the cumin, seasoning to taste and two-thirds of the oil, and pour the mixture into a serving dish. Place in the refrigerator for 2 to 3 hours.

Peel and slice the remaining onion. Heat the remaining oil in a frying pan and sauté the onion, stirring frequently, until crisp and golden brown. Drain on absorbent kitchen paper and arrange the onion slices in small separate mounds on top of the lentil purée. Serve cold.

Coffee Cream

SERVES 6

Egyptian housewives produce mouth-watering desserts to mark festive occasions, such as the celebration of a wedding or a birth in the family. The use of gelatine is a recent innovation; in the old days, a powder made from the root of a plant was used, and many still prefer this traditional method.

300 ml/½ pint single cream
3 egg yolks
75 g/3 oz icing sugar, sifted
15 g/½ oz gelatine
6 tablespoons hot water
3 teaspoons coffee essence
300 ml/½ pint double or whipping cream
175 g/6 oz blanched almonds, roasted

Pour the single cream into a saucepan and bring almost to the boil over a moderate heat, then remove from the heat. Place the egg yolks in a bowl, add the sugar and beat well until thick and light. Gradually stir in the hot cream, blend well and strain the mixture back into the saucepan. Stir for 2 to 3 minutes over a low heat, then remove from the heat.

Dissolve the gelatine in the water in a basin over a saucepan of simmering water. Add the coffee essence and stir the coffee mixture into the warm egg mixture. Blend the ingredients thoroughly and set aside to cool.

Beat the double or whipping cream until thick but not stiff. When the gelatine mixture is cool and beginning to thicken, beat it quickly until light and frothy. Fold in the whipped cream. Wet a 1·15-litre/2-pint mould with cold water and sprinkle the roasted almonds over the bottom. Pour in the coffee cream mixture and chill until set firm. Loosen the edges and turn on to a serving dish. Keep chilled until ready to serve.

Coffee Cream

DOUGHNUTS IN SCENTED SYRUP

SERVES 6

This appears to be a very old recipe, as reference to it can be found in a medieval cookery manual. The Greeks have a similar pastry called *loukoumakes*, as do the Turks, who call it *ickma*. Traditionally, on the fortieth day after a death, these pastries are offered to the neighbours and the poor, as a sign of the ending of the mourning period.

Dough
15 g/½ oz fresh yeast or
10 g/¼ oz dried yeast
1 teaspoon sugar
300 ml/½ pint lukewarm water
450 g/1 lb strong plain flour
300 ml/½ pint milk
Syrup
300 ml/½ pint water
2 tablespoons lemon juice
675 g/1½ lb caster sugar, plus
50-75 g/2-3 oz for coating
2 tablespoons rosewater
2 tablespoons orange-flower water
oil for deep frying
ground cinnamon (optional)

If using fresh yeast, blend the yeast with the sugar and the water and set aside for 10 to 15 minutes or until the liquid becomes frothy. If using dried yeast, sprinkle the yeast over the liquid and leave in a warm place until frothy.

Sift the flour into a mixing bowl and make a well in the centre. Lightly beat the milk into the yeast mixture and pour into the flour, then beat well to form a very soft batter. Cover the bowl and set it aside in a warm place for 1 hour. Beat well, cover the bowl again, and set it aside to rise again for another hour. Repeat this process once or twice more, as thorough beating at regular intervals helps to make the dough very elastic, which gives the doughnuts a perfect round shape.

To make the syrup, pour the water and lemon juice into a heavy saucepan and add the sugar. Bring to the boil over a moderate heat, taking care that the sugar dissolves before boiling point is reached. Lower the heat and simmer until the syrup is thick enough to coat the back of the spoon. Add the rosewater and orange-flower water and simmer for a further 2 to 3 minutes. Remove the saucepan from the heat and set it aside until quite cold.

Heat the oil for deep frying to 190 C/375 F. Beat the batter well and, using a wet teaspoon or a piping bag with a large plain nozzle, drop small amounts of the batter into the hot oil. The doughnuts will rise to the surface quickly. Turn them over and fry them for a further 2 to 3 minutes or until crisp and golden brown. Drain well on absorbent kitchen paper and, while still hot, dip them into the syrup.

Serve hot or cold, with a sprinkling of caster sugar. A little cinnamon may also be sprinkled over if liked.

Doughnuts in Scented Syrup

Greece

There is much controversy about Greek cooking, the main argument being whether it is in fact Greek in origin or Turkish. Certainly there are, at least today, strong similarities between the two cuisines, but this is not surprising since Greece has had a long history of contact with Turkey, including periods of Turkish rule. The Greeks themselves claim a very old culinary tradition, and early writings show that the ancient Greeks took a keen interest in food. Legends about the gods of Mount Olympus recount their preoccupation with the growing of crops and the harvesting of wine, and some gods even gave instructions about the use of ingredients. Such legends reflect the civilisation's dependence on agriculture, and to a large extent this is still true – in Greece there is much less reliance on canned and frozen foods than in Britain or America, and many dishes are seasonal, being made only when the ingredients are available fresh in the markets.

Greek cuisine may not be the most varied or the most sophisticated in the world, and some people find it over-oily, but at its best it is both tasty and satisfying. Even more important, perhaps, is the fact that few Greek dishes are difficult to prepare and cook.

Fish Soup with Lemon Sauce

SERVES 6

(Illustrated on page 11)

The Greeks have been a seafaring nation for thousands of years, so it would have been odd if they had not evolved their own fish soup. The Greek lemon sauce, *avgolemono*, is the same as the Turkish one called *terbiye*.

900 g/2 lb coley, cod, haddock or halibut
2 sticks celery
4 tomatoes
3 medium potatoes, cubed
2 large carrots, roughly chopped
2 large onions, roughly chopped
3-4 large sprigs fresh parsley
3 tablespoons olive oil
1·75 litres/3 pints water
1 tablespoon white wine
1 bay leaf
salt and pepper
50 g/2 oz short-grain rice

Sauce

2 egg yolks
2 tablespoons lemon juice

Remove any bones and skin from the fish and discard them. Rinse the flesh under cold running water and then cut into thick pieces. Cut the celery into 7·5-10 cm/3-4-in pieces. Cover the tomatoes with boiling water, leave for 1 minute and drain. Peel and halve them. Place all the vegetables with the parsley in a large saucepan. Add the oil, water, white wine, bay leaf, and seasoning to taste. Place over a moderate heat and bring to the boil, then reduce the heat and simmer for 20 minutes or until the vegetables are almost cooked. Add the rice and cook for about 30 minutes or until the rice is tender. Add the fish to the pan and cook gently for about 20 to 25 minutes (the pieces of fish should remain whole).

To make the sauce, beat the egg yolks and lemon juice in a small bowl. Gradually add six tablespoons of hot soup taken from the saucepan, stirring constantly. Pour the egg yolk mixture back into the hot soup and, if necessary, reheat to simmering point, but do not boil. Serve immediately.

EASTER SOUP

SERVES 8

In the Greek Orthodox tradition, Easter is a more important festival than Christmas as far as feasting is concerned, and this soup completes the day's celebrations.

1·5 kg/3 lb lamb's tripe, kidney, liver and heart
salt and pepper
50 g/2 oz plain flour
250 ml/8 fl oz cold water
1·75 litres/3 pints lukewarm water
6 spring onions
50 g/2 oz butter or margarine
2 tablespoons chopped fresh parsley
2 tablespoons chopped fresh dill
100 g/4 oz short-grain rice
1 quantity lemon sauce (see Fish Soup with Lemon Sauce, previous page)
2 tablespoons milk

Clean the tripe thoroughly, remove and discard any membrane and gristly parts from the kidney, liver and heart, and rinse all the meats thoroughly under cold running water, then drain. Boil the tripe in salted water for 10 minutes, then drain it and discard the liquid.

Easter Soup

Place it on a board and, when cool enough to handle, cut into very small pieces and place in a large saucepan. Blend the flour to a very soft, smooth paste with the cold water and pour over the tripe. Add the lukewarm water and bring to the boil over a moderate heat, stirring constantly, until the liquid thickens slightly. Part cover the pan, lower the heat and simmer gently for 20 minutes.

Cut the kidney, liver and heart into fairly small pieces, and boil, in salted water to cover, for 5 to 10 minutes. Drain, and discard the liquid. Cut the meat into very small pieces. Chop the spring onions.

Melt the butter in a frying pan, add the kidney, liver, heart, spring onions, parsley and dill and sauté for 5 to 10 minutes, stirring frequently. Add the mixture to the simmering tripe and continue simmering for 20 to 25 minutes or until all the meats are tender. Strain the liquid into a third saucepan and keep the meat warm. Add the rice to the strained liquid, bring to the boil over a moderate heat, then tightly cover the pan and continue to boil for 30 minutes or until the rice is cooked. Remove from the heat. Season to taste.

Make the lemon sauce following the recipe instructions and stir into the soup. Add the meat and, if necessary, reheat the soup to simmering point, but do not boil. Just before serving, add the milk.

Grilled Fish with Olives

SERVES 4

Two staple items of Greek food – fish and olives – which complement each other well, are combined in this recipe to form a truly national dish, with a delicious flavour.

4 trout, mackerel or herrings, about 1 kg/2 lb
Sauce
1 medium onion
5 medium tomatoes
12 stuffed green olives
4 tablespoons olive oil
3 tablespoons pale ale or lager
salt and pepper
Garnish (optional)
1 lemon, quartered
few sprigs parsley

Clean the fish and remove and discard the fins and heads. Rinse under cold running water and leave to drain in a colander.

To make the sauce, peel and thinly slice the onion and tomatoes. Slice the olives. Heat three-quarters of the oil in a frying pan over a moderate heat and sauté the onion until golden brown. Add the tomatoes, olives, pale ale or lager and seasoning to taste, then lower the heat and simmer very gently for 20 to 30 minutes, stirring frequently.

Meanwhile, brush the prepared fish with the remaining oil and grill at a moderate temperature for 5 to 6 minutes on each side, or until the flesh becomes firm and white. Place the fish on a heated serving dish and spoon the sauce over and around them. Garnish with the lemon quarters and the parsley sprigs (if used).

Grilled Fish with Olives

Fish Salad

SERVES 4

This salad is contradictory to all principles of Eastern Mediterranean cooking, as fish and yogurt are not used together in any other dish. The method, however, is Greek, and it is an interesting step in the culinary evolution of the region.

675 g/1 ½ lb cod, haddock, halibut or turbot
salt and pepper
2 hard-boiled eggs
Sauce
4 tablespoons mayonnaise
150 ml/¼ pint natural yogurt
2-3 spring onions
1 tablespoon capers
1 tablespoon chopped fresh dill
salt and pepper

Remove and discard any bones and skin from the fish, rinse under cold running water, and cut into thick pieces. Place the fish in a saucepan, add water to cover and seasoning to taste. Bring to the boil over a moderate heat, then reduce the heat and cook gently for about 20 to 25 minutes. The pieces of fish should remain whole. Drain, allow to cool, then flake the fish into a salad bowl. Shell the eggs and slice them.

To make the sauce, mix together the mayonnaise and yogurt in a bowl. Finely slice the spring onions and add them, with the capers, dill and seasoning to taste. Mix slowly but thoroughly. Spoon the sauce over the fish and garnish the salad with the slices of egg. Serve cold.

Fish Salad

Fish with Garlic Sauce

SERVES 4

In some parts of Turkey, the sauce used in this dish was originally made with hazelnuts. However, almonds are more abundant in Greece and are also considered more of a luxury. This sauce, if made with rather less garlic, is an excellent one to accompany vegetables.

Sauce
1 large potato
4 cloves garlic
1 teaspoon salt
100 g/4 oz ground almonds
6 tablespoons olive oil
3 tablespoons vinegar
4 tablespoons water
little lemon juice
For the fish
4 pieces cod, haddock, halibut or turbot, about 675 g/1 ½ lb
salt and pepper
plain flour for coating
oil for deep-frying

To make the garlic sauce, peel and quarter the potato, place in water to cover, bring to the boil and simmer until tender. Drain and set aside.

Pound the garlic and salt in a mortar or bowl, then add the almonds and potato and continue pounding until a smooth paste is formed. Add the olive oil very gradually, beating well after each addition. Stir in the vinegar and water and mix thoroughly. The mixture should be the consistency of thick mayonnaise. If necessary, add lemon juice until the correct consistency is achieved.

Wipe the pieces of fish with a damp cloth or kitchen paper. Sprinkle it with seasoning to taste, then coat with flour. Heat the oil to 190 C/375 F and deep-fry the fish until crisp and golden brown. Drain on absorbent kitchen paper. Serve hot with the garlic sauce.

Moussaka

SERVES 4-6

2 large aubergines
salt and pepper
2 large onions
about 150 ml/¼ pint olive oil
2 cloves garlic, crushed
675 g/1 ½ lb minced lamb
2 (425-g/15-oz) cans chopped tomatoes
1 tablespoon dried marjoram
300 ml/½ pint natural yogurt
2 eggs, beaten
50 g/2 oz Cheddar cheese, grated
a little grated nutmeg

Trim the ends off the aubergines, then slice them and layer the slices with a generous sprinkle of salt in a colander. Set aside for 30 minutes.

Chop the onions. Heat 2 tablespoons of the oil in a saucepan. Add the onions and garlic and cook until they are soft but not browned. Add the lamb and cook, stirring all the time, until the meat is lightly browned. Pour in the tomatoes, add the marjoram and seasoning to taste. Bring to the boil and remove from the heat.

Wash and dry the aubergine slices. Heat some of the remaining oil in a frying pan and fry the aubergines a few slices at a time, until browned on both sides. Add more oil to the pan as necessary. Drain the aubergines on absorbent kitchen paper. Arrange layers of the aubergines and meat mixture in an ovenproof dish ending with a layer of aubergines.

Beat the yogurt into the eggs with the cheese, a little nutmeg and seasoning. Pour this mixture over the moussaka and bake in a moderate oven (180 C, 350 F, gas 4) for 1 hour or until set and golden on top. Serve at once.

Meat Fingers in Sauce

SERVES 4

This is a very tasty dish. The meat fingers are exceedingly tender, even though they are not cooked for very long.

2 cloves garlic
4 slices white bread
450 g/1 lb minced lean lamb
½ teaspoon dried marjoram
2 eggs, lightly beaten
2 tablespoons plain flour
½ teaspoon salt
pinch pepper
Sauces
1 medium onion
25 g/1 oz butter
15 g/½ oz plain flour
1 tablespoon tomato purée
400 ml/14 fl oz water
salt and pepper
pinch sugar
1 teaspoon chopped fresh parsley
½ teaspoon dried marjoram

Peel and crush the garlic. Remove the crusts from the bread and soak it in a little cold water for 2 minutes, then squeeze out as much water as possible. Place the lamb in a bowl. Add the bread, garlic, marjoram and eggs, and mix thoroughly to a fairly stiff paste. Roll the mixture into finger shapes, about 2·5 cm/1 in thick and 7·5 cm/3 in long. Mix the flour with the salt and the pepper and use to coat the meat fingers.

For the sauce: peel and finely chop the onion. Melt the butter in a saucepan over a moderate heat and sauté the onion until golden brown. Stir in the flour and continue cooking for 1 to 2 minutes, then stir in the tomato purée. Add the water gradually, stirring well all the time. Add the seasoning, sugar, parsley and marjoram, and bring the sauce to the boil, stirring constantly. Lower the heat to a minimum and simmer for 5 minutes. Put the meat fingers one by one into the sauce, and simmer for 10 to 12 minutes. Transfer to a heated serving dish and serve hot with cooked rice and a green salad.

Note: In Egypt, a similar dish is served with a crown of rice around the meat fingers.

Meatcakes with Marjoram

SERVES 4

The marjoram which grows wild on the arid mountain sides in Greece is exceptionally aromatic and imparts a delectable aroma to the meatcakes. Dried marjoram may be used instead.

4 slices white bread
1 egg, lightly beaten
450 g/1 lb finely minced lean lamb
2 teaspoons chopped fresh marjoram
or 1 teaspoon dried marjoram
salt and pepper
flour for coating
100 g/4 oz butter

Remove the crusts from the bread, soak it in cold water for 2 to 3 minutes, then squeeze out the excess moisture. Place the bread in a bowl with the egg, lamb, marjoram and seasoning and mix thoroughly. Knead the mixture very well in the bowl for 5 to 10 minutes until it is a smooth and fairly soft consistency. Divide the mixture into small equal portions, roll each one into a ball about 3·5-5 cm/1½-2 in, and then flatten a little to form a meatcake. Coat the meatcakes in flour.

Melt the butter in a frying pan over a low heat and fry the meatcakes for about 4 minutes on each side until well browned. Drain on absorbent kitchen paper. Serve hot with mashed potatoes, or French fried potatoes, and a green salad.

Ground Almond, Lemon and Cream Dessert

SERVES 4

This easily made dessert is most refreshing on hot summer days.

300 ml/½ pint double or whipping cream
2 teaspoons grated lemon rind
25 g/1 oz ground almonds
3 tablespoons lemon juice
50 g/2 oz caster sugar
4 small pieces candied lemon peel

Place the cream in a bowl, add the lemon rind, ground almonds, lemon juice and sugar and beat until thick and light. Pour the mixture into four serving glasses, and decorate each one with a piece of candied lemon peel. Chill for several hours before serving.

Almond Slices

Almond Slices

MAKES 16-20 PORTIONS

In February, the almond trees of the Greek islands come into flower, the forerunners of spring, which comes early to these parts. Almonds are regarded as a perfect nutrient, and any dish made with almonds is considered both wholesome and refined.

100 g/4 oz butter or margarine
225 g/8 oz caster sugar
4 eggs, lightly beaten
100 g/4 oz ground almonds
1 teaspoon ground cinnamon
225 g/8 oz fine semolina

Syrup

225 g/8 oz caster sugar
300 ml/½ pint water
3 tablespoons lemon juice
50 g/2 oz blanched almonds, split

Cream together the butter or margarine and sugar until soft and creamy. Beat the eggs into the mixture, then add the ground almonds, cinnamon and semolina. Line an 18 × 28-cm/7 × 11-in Swiss roll tin with greased greaseproof paper, allowing the paper to stand about 2·5 cm/1 in higher than the tin. Spread the mixture into the tin, place in the centre of a moderate oven (180 C, 350 F, gas 4) and bake for 1 hour. Remove the tin from the oven and prepare the syrup.

Measure the sugar and water into a saucepan, then stir over a low heat until the sugar has dissolved. Add the lemon juice and bring to the boil. Simmer for 5 minutes until the syrup has reduced slightly. Meanwhile top the cake with the split almonds. Remove the pan from the heat and allow to cool slightly, then pour the hot syrup over the almond cake. Leave to soak until the cake is cool, then cut into squares to serve.

Italy

Italian cooking is immensely varied, not only because it springs from roots as diverse as ancient Greece, Rome, Byzantium and the Orient, but also because the different regions of the country have different climates, agricultures and hence gastronomic traditions. For example, the dishes of the Venetian region (Veneto) are quite different from those of Piedmont, Campania or Liguria, and many products are localised, the best fish being eaten in the coastal regions, the best beef in the cattle-rearing area of Tuscany, the best Parmesan cheese in Parma and so on. The tourist should always try to sample local dishes, since these will undoubtedly be the most rewarding.

But all Italians, from whatever region, have one thing in common – an intense devotion to food and culinary tradition. Italians like to eat as their parents and grandparents did, and consequently recipes are still handed down, guarded and treasured, preserving the country's tradition of fine food.

Salami-Stuffed Pasta in Broth

SERVES 6

Filling
1 small cotechino sausage
75 g/3 oz butter
1 teaspoon chopped carrot
1 teaspoon chopped celery
1 teaspoon chopped onion
350 g/12 oz topside of beef
300 ml/½ pint beef or chicken stock
½ teaspoon salt
pinch pepper
150 g/5 oz toasted fine breadcrumbs
2 tablespoons grated Parmesan cheese
pinch ground nutmeg
3 eggs
Pasta
6 eggs, beaten
1 teaspoon olive oil
450 g/1 lb plain flour
1 teaspoon salt
2·5 litres/4½ pints beef or chicken broth
100 g/4 oz grated Parmesan cheese

Peel the cotechino sausage. Heat the butter in a large saucepan, add the carrot, celery and onion and sauté until lightly browned. Add the cotechino and the beef. Pour in the stock, season to taste, then cover tightly and simmer over a very low heat for 1½ to 2 hours or until the beef is tender and the sauce has thickened. Remove the cotechino and beef and mince finely. Place in a bowl with the sauce and set aside until completely cold, then mix in the breadcrumbs, cheese, nutmeg and eggs.

To make the pasta, lightly whisk together 5 of the eggs and olive oil in a small bowl. Sift the flour and salt into a mixing bowl and make a well in the centre. Pour in the eggs and oil, mix to a smooth dough and knead well. Wrap in a damp cloth and set aside for about 30 minutes. Roll the dough out on a lightly floured surface into two sheets 1 mm/1/16 in thick, and brush with the remaining beaten egg. Arrange small balls of the filling about 3·5 cm/1½ in apart on the first sheet of dough, then cover with the second sheet. Seal in the filling by pressing the spaces between the filling with the fingertips. Using a fluted cutter or a sharp knife, cut out the pasta, and arrange them on a lightly floured surface so that they do not touch. Cook them, a few at a time, in the broth in a large saucepan for 8 to 10 minutes, or until they come to the surface. Serve immediately with the Parmesan cheese sprinkled on top.

Broad Bean Soup

SERVES 6

To count the different minestrones made throughout Italy would be an impossible task. Almost every vegetable grown can be used, so the soup varies both by season and by region. If you prefer, buy the noodles. Pecorino cheese, made from ewe's milk, can be bought at most good delicatessens.

1·5 kg/3 lb unshelled broad beans or
450 g/1 lb frozen broad beans
1 onion
1 carrot
4 sticks celery
50 g/2 oz butter
1·75 litres/3 pints water
4 teaspoons salt
Pasta
5 eggs
1 tablespoon olive oil
450 g/1 lb plain flour
1 teaspoon salt
100 g/4 oz Pecorino cheese, grated to serve

Shell the beans if using fresh ones. Peel and chop the onion and carrot. Chop the celery. Heat the butter in a large saucepan over a moderate heat, add the onion, carrot and celery and sauté until browned. Add the beans, water and salt and bring to the boil. Lower the heat and simmer for 30 to 40 minutes, or until the beans are soft and very tender.

To make the noodles, lightly whisk together the eggs and olive oil in a small bowl. Sift the flour and salt into a mixing bowl and make a well in the centre. Pour in the eggs and the oil, mix to a firm, smooth dough and knead well. Wrap in a damp cloth and set aside for about 30 minutes.

Roll the dough on a floured surface into sheets, each about 20 cm/8 in wide, 30 cm/12 in long and 1 mm/1/16 in thick. Fold each sheet in half lengthways, then in half lengthways again several times. Cut the roll into 5-mm/1/4-in ribbons, then unfold the ribbons, arrange them on a lightly floured surface and allow to dry for about 30 minutes.

Bring the soup back to the boil, add the noodles, and cook for 7 to 8 minutes, or until *al dente* (cooked but still firm). Serve with the cheese.

Broad Bean Soup

Mussel Hot-Pot

SERVES 6

In Taranto, oysters, mussels and other shellfish are cultivated in the centre of the city in the Mar Grande, where they are left to mature for about eighteen months before being caught.

1·75 litres/3 pints mussels
2 tablespoons olive oil
¼ teaspoon freshly ground black pepper
1 small onion
1 clove garlic
450 g/1 lb potatoes
100 g/4 oz bacon fat, minced
2 litres/3½ pints cold water
salt
350 g/12 oz long-grain rice

Scrape and rinse the mussels very thoroughly under running water. Remove and discard the beards. Leave to soak in cold water for 2 hours, then discard any which have opened. Heat 1 tablespoon of olive oil in a saucepan over a moderate heat. Add the mussels and pepper and sauté, shaking the pan frequently, until the mussels open. Discard any which have not opened, as this means they are bad. Drain the rest in a colander over a large bowl and leave to cool. Strain and reserve the liquid. Remove the mussel shells, discard them, and set the mussels aside until required.

Peel and finely chop the onion and garlic. Peel and slice the potatoes. Heat the bacon fat and the remaining tablespoon of olive oil in a flameproof casserole or saucepan over a low heat. Add the onion and garlic and sauté until lightly browned. Add the water and the potatoes, season with salt and bring to the boil. After 10 minutes, add the rice and cook over a high heat for 15 to 20 minutes, adding the mussels and reserved liquid 2 to 3 minutes before the end of the cooking time. Pour into a heated serving dish and serve immediately.

Skewered Scampi with Brandy Sauce

SERVES 6

Mustard was brought to Europe by the travelling Roman soldiers, who mixed the powder with must, or unfermented grape juice. It is from this word that the name was derived.

24 large fresh scampi, peeled, or
24 frozen scampi, thawed
18 bay leaves
salt and freshly ground black pepper
1 tablespoon olive oil

Sauce

2 cloves garlic
6 anchovy fillets
75 g/3 oz butter or margarine
4 tablespoons brandy
a few drops Worcestershire sauce
1 tablespoon French mustard
2 teaspoons lemon juice

Set the oven at moderately hot (190 C, 375 F, gas 5). Using six skewers, thread four scampi and three bay leaves alternately on to each skewer. Season to taste and sprinkle with olive oil. Grease a roasting tin, place the skewers in it, and cook for 15 minutes or until tender and golden brown, brushing occasionally with the juices in the roasting tin and a little more olive oil if necessary. While the scampi are cooking make the sauce.

Peel and crush the garlic. Pound the anchovy fillets with two-thirds of the butter or margarine to make a paste. Heat the remaining butter or margarine in a frying pan over a moderate heat, add the garlic and sauté until lightly browned. Add the brandy and Worcestershire sauce and cook over a high heat until reduced by half. Add the anchovy paste, mustard and lemon juice. Pour the sauce on to an oval heated serving dish and arrange the skewers of scampi on top. Serve very hot.

Stewed Beef with Celery

STEWED BEEF WITH CELERY

SERVES 6

In Rome, where this dish is usually prepared with cardoons, it is called *stufatino al gobbo* 'stew with hunchbacks' since cardoons (gobbi in Italian) droop over at the top. Cardoons are related to the artichoke family, and the stalk is eaten like celery. Since cardoons are rarely available in our shops, celery is used below.

1 kg/2 lb shin of beef
salt and pepper
¼ onion
1 stick celery
75 g/3 oz bacon
15 g/½ oz lard
150 ml/¼ pint dry white wine
150 ml/¼ pint Tomato Sauce (page 42)
1 head celery
1 clove garlic
few sprigs marjoram

Slice the beef and season to taste. Peel and finely chop the onion. Finely chop the celery stick and the bacon. Heat the lard over a moderate heat in a flameproof casserole or a saucepan, add the onion, celery and bacon and sauté until browned. Add the beef and sauté on each side. Pour in the wine and cook until reduced by half, then add the tomato sauce. Continue cooking for 2 to 3 minutes, then add enough water to barely cover the beef, cover the pan tightly and simmer over a low heat for 2 hours or until tender. Add a few tablespoons of hot water to prevent the beef from sticking, if necessary.

Meanwhile, trim the head of celery, wash under cold running water and slice thinly. Cook in boiling salted water until barely tender, then drain well. Peel and chop the garlic, and chop the marjoram. A few minutes before serving, mix the celery with the garlic and marjoram and stir into the beef. Serve hot.

Pot-Roast Beef with Tomato and Wine Sauce

SERVES 6

The wine most used by the Romans in their cooking and for the table is from the Castelli area. Nowadays it is transported to Rome in trucks, but it used to be carried in horse-drawn carts, which filled the roads at night. Each cart held eight 60-litre barrels. Most of the wine is used in the area and little is exported.

1 kg/2 lb top rump or topside of beef
4 cloves garlic
1 teaspoon chopped marjoram
50 g/2 oz bacon fat
salt and freshly ground black pepper
1 medium onion
1 medium carrot
4 sticks celery
575 g/1¼ lb tomatoes
75 g/3 oz ham fat, minced
15 g/½ oz lard
2 teaspoons chopped parsley
pinch grated nutmeg
2-3 cloves
150 ml/¼ pint dry red wine

Make incisions all over the piece of beef with a sharp knife. Peel three of the garlic cloves, chop and mix with the marjoram. Cut the bacon fat into fine strips, roll in the garlic mixture, then season the strips with the salt and pepper and press into the incisions in the beef. Peel and slice the onion and carrot and slice the celery. Peel and chop the remaining garlic. Cover the tomatoes with boiling water, leave for 1 minute. Drain and peel them. Purée them in a liquidiser.

Heat the ham fat and lard in a saucepan over a moderate heat. Add the onion, carrot, celery, garlic and parsley. Tie the meat with fine string to maintain its shape during the cooking and place in the saucepan. Sauté until browned, then add the nutmeg and the cloves. Season with salt and pepper. Pour in the wine and cook over a high heat until reduced to 2 tablespoons, then add the tomatoes with enough water to barely cover the beef. Cover the saucepan tightly and simmer over a moderate heat for 2 hours or until tender. Remove the beef from the saucepan, remove and discard the string and carve into slices. Arrange on a heated serving plate and keep hot. Reduce the sauce until fairly thick and strain it over the meat. Serve very hot.

Meat Sauce

MAKES 450 ml / ¾ pint

This is probably the best-known Italian sauce – if it is well made with the very best ingredients, it is a perfect accompaniment to pasta dishes.

25 g/1 oz butter
½ small onion, chopped
½ small carrot, chopped
1 small clove garlic, peeled and chopped
1 small stick celery, chopped
2 tablespoons olive oil
50 g/2 oz ham or lean bacon, chopped
3 dried mushrooms, soaked, drained and chopped
225 g/8 oz coarsely minced beef
5 tablespoons dry red wine
sprig parsley
sprig marjoram
salt and pepper
2 teaspoons plain flour
4 tomatoes, peeled and chopped

Heat the butter in a frying pan over a moderate heat, add the onion, carrot, garlic and celery and sauté until lightly browned. Remove the frying pan from the heat and set aside. Heat the olive oil in a saucepan over a moderate heat, add the ham and sauté until lightly browned. Add the onion mixture, mushrooms and beef. Cook for 10 to 15 minutes over a moderate heat, then pour the wine over the ingredients. Chop the parsley and marjoram together, add to the frying pan and season with salt and pepper.

When the wine is reduced to 1 teaspoon, remove the frying pan from the heat and stir in the flour. Mix thoroughly, then return to the heat and cook the mixture very gently for 10 to 15 minutes, stirring constantly. Add the tomatoes and cook, adding 1 tablespoon of water occasionally to prevent the sauce from sticking. Remove the frying pan from the heat as soon as the sauce is well blended and slightly thickened.

Veal with Tuna Sauce

SERVES 6

In Italy, veal from a young milk-fed calf is used for this dish, but older veal may be substituted. Surprisingly, the fish sauce blends perfectly with veal.

8 anchovy fillets
3 tablespoons milk
1 medium onion
2 medium carrots
6 gherkins
1 stick celery
½ lemon
1 piece boned and rolled breast of veal, about 1·25 kg/2½ lb
150 ml/¼ pint dry white wine
3 tablespoons olive oil
300 ml/½ pint cold water

Sauce

1 (200-g/7-oz) tin tuna in oil
2 anchovy fillets
4 egg yolks
450 ml/¾ pint olive oil
3 tablespoons lemon juice
salt and pepper

Garnish

2 tablespoons capers
3 pickled onions

Soak the anchovy fillets in the milk for 10 to 15 minutes to remove the excess salt. Drain, and discard the milk. Peel and slice the onion and one of the carrots. Peel the remaining carrot and cut into thick strips. Cut the gherkins in half lengthways. Slice the celery. Thinly pare the rind from the half lemon and squeeze the lemon to extract the juice.

Using a sharp knife, make small incisions in the veal and insert the anchovy fillets. Tie the strips of carrot and the gherkins around the veal with thin clean string. Place the veal in a flameproof casserole or large saucepan together with the sliced onion, carrot and celery. Add the lemon rind and juice, wine, olive oil and water, cover and cook over a moderate heat for about 2 hours or until tender. Remove the pan from the heat and lift out the veal, removing and discarding the string, gherkins and carrots. Place the veal in a bowl and strain the stock over it, then set aside to cool. When cold, pour the stock into a small saucepan and boil rapidly over high heat until reduced to about 4 tablespoons. Remove from the heat and set aside until required.

To make the sauce, drain the excess oil from the tuna and pound it together with the anchovy fillets to form a paste. Dilute this with 3 tablespoons of the reserved veal stock and press through a fine sieve, or blend in a liquidiser. Place the egg yolks in a mixing bowl or blender and add the olive oil drop by drop, beating constantly until a thick mayonnaise is formed. Add the lemon juice and gradually stir in the fish purée. The sauce should be of a thick pouring consistency; if too thick add the remaining veal stock. Add salt to taste.

Thinly slice the veal and place on a serving dish. Coat with some of the fish sauce and garnish with the capers and pickled onions. Serve cold with the remaining sauce.

Veal with Tuna Sauce

Stuffed Pasta with Walnut Sauce

SERVES 6

The walnut sauce is a speciality of Liguria and the fat little squares of ravioli with which it is served are known as *pansôti*.

Filling
50 g/2 oz lamb's brains
50 g/2 oz lamb's sweetbreads
350 g/12 oz spinach
225 g/8 oz beetroot leaves
225 g/8 oz fresh borage
225 g/8 oz watercress
50 g/2 oz butter or margarine
150 g/5 oz Ricotta cheese
2 eggs, beaten
1 clove garlic, crushed
pinch ground nutmeg
salt
Pasta
5 eggs
2 tablespoons warm water
675 g/1½ lb plain flour
1 teaspoon salt
Sauce
1 clove garlic
100 g/4 oz shelled walnuts
50 g/2 oz pine-nut kernels
about 150 ml/¼ pint olive oil
100 g/4 oz Parmesan cheese, grated

Soak the brains and sweetbreads in cold water for 1 hour, then blanch them in boiling water, drain well and remove any skin, blood vessels and coarse tissue. Rinse the spinach, beetroot leaves, borage (if you cannot get borage use extra spinach as an alternative) and watercress under cold running water. Remove and discard any tough stems, and shred all the leaves. Cook in lightly salted boiling water until tender, then drain thoroughly and press through a sieve (or blend in a liquidiser) into a large bowl. Heat the butter or margarine in a frying pan over a moderate heat and sauté the brains and sweetbreads for 5 to 6 minutes, stirring frequently. Blend in a liquidiser, or press through a sieve, then add to the puréed greens.

Sieve the Ricotta cheese and stir into the brain mixture, with the eggs and garlic. Add the nutmeg, season to taste, and mix to a stiff paste. With floured hands, roll the paste into small balls, each about the size of a walnut, and set aside while making the pasta.

To make the pasta, lightly whisk together 4 eggs with the water in a small bowl. Sift the flour and salt into a mixing bowl and make a well in the centre. Pour in the eggs and water, mix to a firm, smooth dough and knead well. Wrap the dough in a damp cloth and set aside for about 30 minutes. Roll the dough out on a floured surface into two sheets about 1 mm/1/16 in thick. Beat the remaining egg and brush the first sheet with beaten egg. Place the balls of filling about 5 cm/2 in apart on the first sheet of dough, cover with the second sheet and press firmly between the rounds of filling to seal the two layers together. Using a fluted pastry wheel or a sharp knife, cut out the ravioli into 5-cm/2-in squares. Leave on a floured surface until required.

To make the sauce, peel the garlic and chop or mince it together with the walnuts and pine-nut kernels. Press the mixture through a sieve into a bowl, or purée in a liquidiser or food processor. Add the olive oil drop by drop, beating constantly as though making a mayonnaise, until a thick coating mixture is formed. Add more oil if necessary. Place a few ravioli at a time in a large saucepan half filled with lightly salted boiling water, and simmer for about 15 minutes. Remove with a perforated spoon and drain well. Place the ravioli on a heated serving dish, sprinkle with the Parmesan cheese and cover with the walnut sauce, then mix well, and place in a moderately hot oven (200 C, 400 F, gas 6) for 5 to 10 minutes. Serve immediately.

White Sauce

MAKES 300 ml/½ pint

15 g/½ oz butter or margarine
15 g/½ oz plain flour
300 ml/½ pint milk or chicken stock
salt and pepper

Melt the butter or margarine in a saucepan. Add the flour and cook gently stirring all the time for 2 minutes. Gradually pour in the liquid, stirring, and bring to the boil. Simmer for 2-3 minutes. Season to taste.

Macaroni with Bacon and Tomato

SERVES 6

175 g/6 oz very lean bacon rashers
1 kg/2 lb tomatoes
¼ onion
2 tablespoons olive oil
1 tablespoon dry white wine
1 fresh basil leaf or pinch dried basil
1 small chilli
salt and pepper
575 g/1 ¼ lb macaroni
100 g/4 oz grated Pecorino or Parmesan cheese

To make a tomato sauce, cut the bacon into 2·5-cm/1-in pieces. Plunge the tomatoes into boiling water for 1 minute, remove then peel and finely slice them. Peel and chop the onion. Heat the olive oil in a heavy frying pan over a high heat and sauté the bacon until browned, then drain and keep hot. Pour the wine into the frying pan, then add the onion, basil and whole chilli. When the onion is lightly browned, add the tomatoes and salt to taste. Stir for 8 to 10 minutes. Remove and discard the chilli and the basil leaf, if used, add the bacon and simmer very gently for 10 to 15 minutes.

Meanwhile, break the pasta into 7·5-cm/3-in pieces and cook in plenty of lightly salted boiling water for about 10 minutes or until *al dente* (cooked but still firm). Drain, turn on to a large heated serving plate and cover with half the cheese and the tomato sauce. Mix well and serve with the remaining cheese.

Note: Authentic macaroni is similar in length to spaghetti and it is often (as for this recipe) broken up before eating. Short-cut macaroni can be substituted if you like.

Macaroni with Bacon and Tomato

Spinach Lasagne

SERVES 6

Styles of pasta cooking vary widely, particularly from north to south. The northern regions in particular specialise in Pasta Bolognese (meat sauce) and the flat ribbon-type noodles are made at home, usually with eggs, whereas people in the south normally buy dried Pasta Napoletana, a macaroni which is sometimes made without eggs.

225 g/8 oz fresh spinach or
225 g/8 oz frozen chopped spinach, thawed and thorougly drained
2 eggs
1 tablespoon olive oil
450 g/1 lb flour
1 teaspoon salt
450 ml/¾ pint Meat Sauce (page 32)
150 ml/¼ pint White Sauce (page 34)
175 g/6 oz Parmesan cheese, grated
100-175 g/4-6 oz butter, melted
1 black truffle (optional)

Rinse the fresh spinach under cold running water and drain well. Cook in very little boiling salted water for about 10 minutes, or until soft. Drain very well. Chop finely, purée in a liquidiser or press through a sieve, and set aside until cold. Lightly whisk together the eggs and olive oil in a small bowl. Sift the flour and salt into a mixing bowl and make a well in the centre. Pour in the eggs and olive oil, add the spinach and mix to a smooth dough, kneading well until the mixture is evenly coloured. Wrap in a damp cloth and set aside for about 30 minutes.

Roll the dough into three sheets about 1 mm/1⁄16 in thick, and cut into 7·5-cm/3-in squares. Cook six to eight of the squares at a time in a shallow pan half filled with lightly salted boiling water for 3 to 4 minutes, then remove with a perforated spoon, drain well and set aside to cool on a damp cloth. Butter a 1·75 litre/3-pint ovenproof casserole and arrange the pasta in layers, covering each layer with 3 tablespoons of the meat sauce, then white sauce, then grated cheese and butter. Sprinkle the top with cheese and butter only. Place in a moderate oven (180C, 350F, gas 4) for 20 to 30 minutes or until the surface is well browned. Slice the truffle, if using, and garnish with it. Serve immediately with any remaining cheese.

Ribbon Noodles with Ricotta Cheese

SERVES 6

Ricotta, being a particular favourite of the Romans, is served quite often with pasta in this way. The cheese, mainly made from ewes' milk, is unsalted, but may be salted, smoked or eaten with sugar and cinnamon as a dessert. The noodles can be bought ready-made if you prefer.

Pasta
5 eggs
1 tablespoon olive oil
450 g/1 lb plain flour
1 teaspoon salt
Topping
350 g/12 oz Ricotta cheese
3-4 tablespoons olive oil
salt and pepper

To make the pasta, lightly whisk together the eggs and olive oil in a small bowl. Sift the flour and salt into a mixing bowl and make a well in the centre. Pour in the eggs and the oil, mix to a firm smooth dough and knead well. Wrap in a damp cloth and set aside for about 30 minutes.

Roll the dough out on a floured surface into sheets about 20 cm/12 in long and 1 mm/1⁄16 in thick. Fold each sheet in half lengthways, then in half lengthways again, several times. Cut the roll into 5-mm/¼-in ribbon noodles, then unfold the noodles, arrange them on a floured surface and allow them to dry for about 30 minutes. Place the noodles in a large saucepan half filled with lightly salted boiling water and simmer for about 8 minutes, or until *al dente* (cooked but still firm). Drain and place on a heated serving plate, reserving the cooking water.

Press the Ricotta cheese through a sieve over the noodles, sprinkle with olive oil and a little of the water in which the noodles were cooked, if necessary, to moisten. Add salt and pepper to taste. Mix together and serve.

Tuna Pizza

SERVES 4

Pizza Dough
2 teaspoons dried yeast
about 150 ml/¼ pint tepid water
175 g/6 oz strong plain flour
¼ teaspoon salt
Topping
1 onion, chopped
1 (425-g/15-oz) can tomatoes, drained
1 (198-g/7-oz) can tuna, drained
salt and pepper
2 tablespoons each chopped fresh parsley and basil
2 tablespoons olive oil

Sprinkle the yeast over the water, stir lightly until frothy. Sift the flour and salt into a bowl. Stir in the yeast liquid to make a smooth dough. Turn the dough out on to a floured board and knead well until smooth and elastic. Leave in a warm place until doubled in size.

Turn the risen dough out on to a floured surface, knock back lightly then shape into a large thin pizza (about 30 cm/12 in across) and place on a greased baking tray. Sprinkle the onion over the dough, then top with the tomatoes, tuna, olives, seasoning and herbs. Sprinkle gently with oil and bake in a very hot oven (240 C, 475 F, gas 9) for about 20 minutes or until the base is golden. Serve at once.

Tuna Pizza

TRAY PIZZA

SERVES 6-8

double quantity pizza dough
(see Tuna Pizza, previous page)
Topping
2 (425-g/15-oz) cans tomatoes, drained
salt and pepper
2 cloves garlic, finely chopped
450 g/1 lb mozzarella cheese, coarsely grated
2 (50-g/2-oz) cans anchovies, drained
2 tablespoons chopped fresh basil or parsley to garnish
black olives to serve (optional)

Make the pizza dough according to the recipe instructions, then roll it out to line a greased 23 × 33-cm/9 × 13-in baking tray or Swiss roll tin.

Top the pizza with the tomatoes, sprinkle with seasoning and the garlic. Cover with a thick layer of cheese. Cut the anchovies in half lengthways, then arrange the pieces on top of the pizza and bake in a hot oven (240 C, 475 F, gas 9) for about 20 minutes or until lightly browned. Sprinkle with chopped basil or parsley just before serving and offer a bowl of olives with the pizza.

Variations

Mushroom pizza: Add 225 g/8 oz thinly sliced mushrooms, laying them on top of the tomatoes before adding the cheese.

Pepper pizza: Deseed and chop 2-3 red and green peppers and sprinkle them over the tomatoes before adding the cheese.

Tray Pizza

AUBERGINE PIZZA

SERVES 4

I quantity pizza dough (see Tuna Pizza, page 37)
Topping
2 medium aubergines
salt and pepper
4 tablespoons olive oil
2 (425-g/15-oz) cans tomatoes, drained
2 cloves garlic, chopped
225 g/8 oz mozzarella cheese, sliced
I tablespoon each chopped fresh basil and parsley

Prepare the dough according to the recipe instructions.

For the topping trim the aubergines and cut them into cubes. Place in a colander, sprinkle with salt and leave to drain for 30 minutes. Rinse well and dry the cubes. Heat the oil in a large frying pan, add the aubergines and cook for a few minutes, stirring frequently. Remove the pan from the heat.

Roll out the pizza dough into a 30-cm/12-in round and place it on a greased baking tray. Top with the tomatoes, aubergines with all the oil and cheese. Sprinkle with the herbs and bake in a hot oven (240 C, 475 F, gas 9) for about 20 minutes. Serve immediately.

PIZZA MARGHERITA

SERVES 4

(Illustrated on page 13)
I quantity pizza dough (see Tuna Pizza, page 37)
Topping
2 (425-g/15-oz) cans tomatoes, drained
salt and pepper
I tablespoon chopped fresh basil
225 g/8 oz mozzarella cheese, sliced
2 tablespoons grated Parmesan cheese
2 tablespoons olive oil
a few fresh basil leaves to garnish

Make the pizza dough according to the recipe instructions. Roll it out into a 30-cm/12-in pizza and place it on a greased baking tray. Top with the tomatoes, seasoning, basil and mozzarella. Sprinkle with the Parmesan and olive oil, then bake in a hot oven (240 C, 475 F, gas 9) for 20 minutes or until golden. Garnish with basil leaves and serve.

Aubergine Pizza

LIGURIAN CHICK PEA PUDDING

SERVES 6

In some parts of Italy, chick-pea flour is used to make a thick pancake, fried in oil. In this recipe, the mixture is covered with oil and cooked in the oven.

2 litres/3½ pints cold water
675 g/1½ lb chick pea flour
2 teaspoons salt
250 ml/8 fl oz olive oil
freshly milled black pepper

Pour the water into a large saucepan and place over a moderate heat. Gradually sprinkle in the chick pea flour, stirring constantly with a wooden spoon, until the mixture thinly coats the back of the spoon. Season with salt then reduce the heat and simmer for about an hour, stirring and skimming occasionally.

Grease a 23 × 33·5-cm/9 × 13-in roasting tin or dish with a little of the olive oil and pour in the chick pea mixture. It should be about 2·5 cm/1 in deep. Pour the remaining olive oil over the pudding so that it thinly covers the surface. Place in a moderately hot oven (200 C, 400 F, gas 6) and cook for about 45 minutes, or until the surface is golden brown and crisp. Just before serving, sprinkle with pepper. Serve hot or cold.

POTATO GNOCCHI WITH MEAT SAUCE

SERVES 6

Gnocchi are made all over Italy and seem to have no particular home, but the version made around Rome uses potato rather than flour or semolina.

2 kg/4 lb potatoes
about 450 g/1 lb plain flour
2 teaspoons salt
450 ml/¾ pint Meat Sauce (page 32)
100 g/4 oz butter
150 g/5 oz Parmesan cheese, grated

Cook the potatoes unpeeled in lightly salted water until barely tender, then drain and peel them. Press through a sieve or purée in a food processor and place in a mixing bowl. While still warm, make a well in the centre, add the flour and salt, and mix to form a soft dough, adding a little more flour if necessary. Knead lightly until smooth. Divide the dough into pieces and, with floured hands, form into long rolls, about 2·5 cm/1 in. in diameter. Cut the rolls into 3·5-cm/1½-in pieces and make a lengthwise groove on either side of each piece by pressing between the index and second fingers. Arrange them on a lightly floured surface, making sure that they do not touch, and set aside for 10 to 15 minutes to dry.

To cook, place a few gnocchi at a time into a large saucepan half filled with lightly salted boiling water. As soon as they come to the surface, remove them with a perforated spoon, drain well and place on a large heated serving dish and keep warm. When all the gnocchi are cooked, heat the meat sauce and pour half of it over them, then dot the surface with pieces of butter and sprinkle with one-third of the cheese. Serve very hot, accompanied with the remaining hot meat sauce and cheese.

TOMATO SAUCE

SERVES 4

2 onions
1 clove garlic
25 g/1 oz butter
1 teaspoon dried basil
1 (425-g/15-oz) can chopped tomatoes
150 ml/¼ pint chicken stock or red wine
1 bay leaf
2 tablespoons tomato purée
salt and pepper

Peel and chop the onions and garlic. Melt the butter in saucepan. Fry the onion and garlic until soft but not browned. Stir in the basil, tomatoes, stock or wine, bay leaf and tomato purée. Bring to the boil and simmer for 5 minutes. Season to taste. Discard the bay leaf before serving.

EASTER CAKES

SERVES 6

Dough
75 g/3 oz fresh yeast or
40 g/1 ½ oz dried yeast
1 teaspoon caster sugar
175 ml/6 fl oz lukewarm milk
550 g/19 oz plain flour
4 eggs, beaten
100 g/4 oz caster sugar
100 g/4 oz lard, butter or margarine
2 tablespoons orange-flower water
pinch salt
little warm milk for mixing
Decoration
6 eggs
1 egg yolk, beaten
25 g/1 oz caster sugar

Blend the fresh yeast with the sugar and the milk or sprinkle the dried yeast over the surface of the milk and sugar and leave in a warm place until frothy. Sift 75 g/3 oz of the flour into a mixing bowl and make a well in the centre, then pour in the yeast mixture and mix to a soft dough. Place in a lightly floured bowl, cover and set aside in a warm place for about 1 ½ hours or until doubled in size.

To make the dough, sift the remaining flour into a mixing bowl and make a well in the centre. Add the yeast mixture, eggs, sugar, lard, orange-flower water and salt. Mix the ingredients together to form a soft dough, adding a little warm milk if necessary. Knead for about 30 minutes or until very smooth and well blended. Take about one-tenth of the dough, cover and set aside. Divide the remaining dough into two portions and place in two 1·75-litre/3-pint ring moulds. The mixture should half fill the moulds. Cover and set aside in a warm place for 3 or 4 hours, or until doubled in size.

For the decoration, gently press three whole eggs, evenly spaced, into the dough in each mould. Make small rolls, each about 7·5 cm/3 in long and 5 mm/¼ in wide, from the reserved dough. Place four rolls in a crisscross pattern over each egg, pressing the ends firmly into position. Brush the surface of the dough with the egg yolk blended with a little water, then sprinkle with the sugar. Place in a moderate oven (160 C, 325 F, gas 3) and bake for about 50 to 60 minutes or until well risen and golden brown. Remove from the moulds when cool and leave to cool completely on a wire rack.

CARAMELISED ORANGES

SERVES 6

12 oranges
175 g/6 oz sugar
100 ml/4 fl oz water

Thinly pare the rind from 1 orange and cut it into fine strips. Cook the strips of orange rind in boiling water for 2-3 minutes, or until softened and drain well. Cut all the peel and pith off the oranges and put them in a heatproof bowl.

Put the sugar and water in a saucepan and heat gently, stirring, until the sugar dissolves. Bring to the boil and boil hard until the syrup changes to a golden caramel. Do not allow the caramel to become too dark as it will continue to cook after the pan is removed from the heat. Pour the caramel over the oranges and leave to cool then chill overnight. Transfer to a glass dish and serve with whipped cream.

Caramelised Oranges

Lebanon

At the end of the First World War, Lebanon broke away from the Ottoman Empire, and from that period until it became the battle-scarred wilderness it is today, the country was noted for its fine cooking. Lebanese cuisine, although based on that of Istanbul, included some special national creations which were neither variants nor interpretations of Turkish dishes, but originated from the high, mountainous environment itself. The country was famous for its fruit, particularly cherries, plums, apricots and bananas, and the art of making fresh-fruit ice cream was perfected in a particular shop in Beirut's main square, while a nearby shop was famed for its version of baklava, filled with the luscious apricots from the nearby groves.

Grilled Fresh Sardines

SERVES 4

Just above Beirut's largest beach there used to be, in more peaceful times, numerous small restaurants that specialised in grilled sardines. This is a typical dish and ideal for a picnic. It should be cooked over charcoal on a barbecue, but can be grilled instead.

16-24 small fresh sardines or sprats
salt
2 lemons, cut into wedges

Scale and clean the fish and rinse under cold running water. Spike them through the neck on to the skewers, taking care not to damage the flesh. Sprinkle with salt to taste and grill or barbecue until the skins are charred and the flesh is firm and white. Serve garnished with the lemon wedges and with Onion Salad (page 73).

Grilled Fresh Sardines

Rice and Fish

SERVES 4 to 6

Sayda, the ancient city of Sidon, is perched on the edge of the sea with a hinterland of orange groves, and when the trees are in flower, the air is filled with the scent. This rice and fish dish was traditionally prepared at picnics in these orange groves, now, alas, a thing of the past.

225 g/8 oz whitebait or small sprats
1 large onion
75 g/3 oz butter or margarine
225 g/8 oz long-grain rice
1 ½ teaspoons fresh thyme or
½ teaspoon dried thyme
salt and pepper

Rinse the fish under cold running water and drain thoroughly. Peel and finely chop the onion. Melt the butter or margarine in a large heavy saucepan over a moderate heat, add the onion and sauté until lightly browned. Add the fish and sauté until just beginning to brown, then add the rice and stir gently until the grains become opaque. Stir in the thyme and seasoning to taste. Remove from the heat and gradually stir in the water. After each addition, push the spoon across the bottom of the saucepan from the near side toward the opposite side. When enough water has been added, the rice will form a peak just above the surface of the liquid, about three-quarters of the way across the pan. Bring to the boil, then cover the pan tightly and cook the rice for 25 minutes. Remove the lid and stir the rice gently with a wooden spoon, starting from the edges and heaping the rice into a cone in the centre. Replace the lid and leave the saucepan over a low heat for a further 5 minutes, then take off the lid and let the rice stand for 3 minutes. Serve on a heated plate, heaped into a cone shape.

Lebanese Meatballs with Yogurt Sauce

SERVES 6

This is one of the richer Lebanese dishes for special occasions. The local flat bread is served with it to mop up the delicious sauce.

225 g/8 oz finely minced lean lamb
225 g/8 oz cracked wheat (bulghur wheat)
salt and pepper
25 g/1 oz plain flour
600 ml/1 pint lamb or beef stock
900 ml/1 ½ pints natural yogurt
1 teaspoon finely chopped fresh parsley
1 teaspoon finely chopped fresh mint

Reduce the lamb to a fine pulp, using a food processor or pestle and mortar. Pound or grind the cracked wheat in the same way to a fine gritty consistency, then mix the lamb and wheat together and add seasoning to taste. Divide the mixture into 24 small portions and roll into meatballs each about 3·5 cm/1 ½ in. in diameter.

Blend the flour to a smooth paste in a large heavy saucepan with a little of the meat stock. Gradually add the remaining stock and bring the liquid to the boil over a moderate heat, stirring constantly until it thickens slightly. Simmer for 5 minutes, then add the meatballs and simmer for 20 minutes, or until they rise to the surface.

Beat the yogurt in a bowl with the parsley, mint and seasoning to taste. Stir into the simmering stock for the last 3 minutes of cooking. Pour the mixture into a heated soup tureen and serve hot.

Lentil and Cracked Wheat Salad

SERVES 4

This is one of the healthiest and most delicious Lebanese dishes. The salad is eaten raw, thereby retaining all its rich store of vitamins.

100 g/4 oz red lentils
100 g/4 oz cracked wheat (bulghur wheat)
1 large onion
2 green peppers
4 medium tomatoes
1 tablespoon chopped fresh dill or 2 teaspoons dried dill
1 teaspoon chopped fresh mint
1 tablespoon chopped fresh parsley
3 tablespoons lemon juice
3 tablespoons olive oil
salt and pepper

Soak the lentils and cracked wheat separately in plenty of cold water for 48 hours, changing the water several times. Drain well.

Peel and finely chop the onion. Halve and remove the seeds from the peppers and tomatoes, and chop them into 5-mm/¼-in pieces. Mix the lentils, cracked wheat, onion, peppers, tomatoes, dill, mint, parsley, lemon juice, oil and seasoning to taste together in a large bowl and leave to stand overnight.

Serve the salad cold, with warmed crusty bread or pitta bread.

Little Domes

SERVES 4 to 5

These little *kibbas* are eaten either by themselves or with a salad. They were often taken out on picnic lunches.

225 g/8 oz lean lamb cut from the leg or the same quantity minced lamb
¼ teaspoon dried thyme
¼ teaspoon dried marjoram
225 g/8 oz cracked wheat (bulghur wheat)
1 large onion
50 g/2 oz butter or margarine
1 teaspoon pine-nut kernels
salt and pepper
oil for deep-frying
few sprigs parsley

Reduce the lamb to a smooth pulp in a food processor or with a pestle and mortar. Add half the thyme and marjoram and set aside until required. Grind or pound the cracked wheat in the same way to a fine gritty consistency.

Peel and finely chop the onion. Heat the butter or margarine in a frying pan over a moderate heat, add the onion, sauté it until it is soft and when the onion is just beginning to brown, add the pine-nut kernels and continue to sauté until both are well browned. Remove the pan from the heat, stir in the remaining thyme and marjoram and season to taste.

Mix together the lamb and cracked wheat and squeeze the mixture together with the hands until thoroughly mixed. Divide the lamb mixture into 24 small portions, shape each one into a ball and make a hollow in the centre. Place a little less than a teaspoon of the onion and nut mixture into the hollow, then seal up the opening, completely enclosing the filling and shape into domes. Heat the oil to 190C/375F and deep-fry the domes, then drain on kitchen paper. Arrange the domes on a serving dish and garnish with sprigs of parsley. Serve either hot or cold.

Lentil and Cracked Wheat Salad

Tray Kibba

Tray Kibba

SERVES 4

This *kibba*, a simpler version of one called *kibba Lebaniya*, might be described as a Mediterranean meat loaf.

225 g/8 oz finely minced lean lamb
225 g/8 oz cracked wheat (bulghur wheat)
salt and pepper
Filling
1 large onion
100 g/4 oz butter or margarine
1 teaspoon fresh thyme or ½ teaspoon dried thyme
1 teaspoon pine-nut kernels

Reduce the lamb to a fine pulp, using a food processor or pestle and mortar. Pound or grind the cracked wheat in the same way to a fine gritty consistency. Mix the lamb and wheat together and add seasoning to taste.

To prepare the filling, peel and finely chop the onion. Melt half the butter or margarine in a small saucepan over a moderate heat, add the onion and sauté until soft and golden brown. Remove from the heat and stir in the thyme and pine-nut kernels.

Spread half the lamb mixture in a small roasting pan, cover with the filling, then spread the remaining lamb mixture over the filling. Cut the remaining butter or margarine into small cubes and place on top. Place in a moderately hot oven (190C, 375F, gas 5) for 40 minutes. Cut into squares in the pan, and serve hot as a main dish with a green salad or vegetable.

Baklava

MAKES 12

Rich pastries such as baklava are common to all Eastern Mediterranean countries.

350 g/12 oz blanched almonds
225 g/8 oz butter
about 12 large sheets phylo pastry
Syrup
450 ml/15 fl oz water
2 teaspoons lemon juice
350 g/12 oz caster sugar
5-cm/2-in piece cinnamon stick

Toast the almonds until lightly browned, then chop them coarsely. Melt the butter. Cut the pastry into 23-cm/9-in squares.

Using a little of the melted butter, grease a deep 23-cm/9-in baking tray or meat pan and place one square of pastry in the bottom. Brush the pastry layer with a little of the melted butter and sprinkle it with chopped almonds. Cover with a second layer of pastry. Continue in this way until all the pastry and almonds and most of the butter have been used. Brush the top layer of pastry well with melted butter. With a sharp knife, mark the top of the *baklava* into 12 oblong pieces. Bake in a moderate oven (180C, 350F, gas 4) for 45 minutes or until the *baklava* is golden brown. Remove the tray from the oven and set it aside to cool.

To make the syrup, place the water, lemon juice, sugar and cinnamon stick in a small heavy saucepan and heat slowly until the sugar has completely dissolved. Bring to the boil, lower the heat and simmer for 5 minutes. Pour the hot syrup over the cold *baklava* and set aside until the syrup is cold. Cut along the marks made before baking and serve as required.

Spain

The most famous recipe from Spain must be paella – a colourful dish of rice flavoured with saffron and mixed with a variety of vegetables, seafood and chicken. Other well-known specialities from this part of the Mediterranean include gazpacho, stuffed peppers or tomatoes and, of course, dishes using large Spanish onions.

One easy and quite delicious traditional recipe is Spanish omelette – a simple potato and onion omelette. The common variation includes all sorts of vegetables and a recipe for this is included in this Chapter. The selection of recipes on the following pages include many which are the most famous of Mediterranean dishes.

CHILLED VEGETABLE SOUP

SERVES 6

Known as Gazpacho, this is one of the classic dishes of Andalusia. Before blenders and food processors existed, the operation of cutting up the ingredients as minutely as possible was done by hand. Even today many classically minded cooks defend the old system, but many modern housewives do use mechanical methods for the preparation. Gazpacho must be served very cold and may be eaten either at the beginning of a meal or at the end.

2 cloves garlic
pinch cumin
1 kg/2 lb ripe tomatoes or
2 (425-g/14-oz) cans tomatoes
2 medium onions
½ large cucumber
2 large green peppers
3 thick slices white bread
5 tablespoons olive oil
3 teaspoons salt
6 tablespoons wine vinegar
1 litre/2 pints water

Peel the garlic and pound to a paste with the cumin in a bowl or mortar. Drop the tomatoes into boiling water for 1 minute, remove then peel and coarsely chop them with the onions and cucumber. Remove and discard the seeds from the peppers and chop the flesh. Soak the bread in cold water for about 30 seconds; then squeeze out the excess moisture.

Place three-quarters of the chopped vegetables in a blender with the garlic paste, bread and oil, and reduce to a purée, or chop finely by hand, then pour into a bowl, stir in the salt, vinegar and water and chill thoroughly. Very finely chop the remaining vegetables and place in small bowls. Serve the gazpacho very cold in deep soup bowls or cups. Each diner helps himself to the vegetables of his choice from the small bowls.

SOUSED TROUT

SERVES 6

Marinated trout is best eaten cold, two or three days after pickling. It is best made with freshly caught trout, a fish which is abundant in the north and the centre of Spain. The ideal ones for this dish weigh about 350 g/12 oz each.

6 trout
1½ teaspoons salt
50 g/2 oz plain flour
4 tablesppons olive oil
2 cloves garlic
4 bay leaves
generous 450 ml/¾ pint wine vinegar

Clean the trout and cut off and discard the heads, fins and tails. Rinse under cold running water and dry well. Cut each fish into four to six portions, sprinkle with salt, and coat with flour. Heat half the oil in a frying pan and sauté the pieces of fish until golden brown. Drain and place in a flameproof casserole or saucepan.

Peel and finely chop the garlic. Heat the remaining oil in the pan and sauté the garlic and bay leaves for 3 to 4 minutes. Add the vinegar and simmer for 10 minutes, then pour over the fish pieces, making sure they are completely covered. Bring to the boil, then lower the heat and simmer for 5 minutes. Remove from the heat and set aside until cold. Serve two or three days after pickling, or store in airtight jars or bottles until required.

Baked Scallops

SERVES 4

The scallop is one of the great delicacies of Galician gastronomy. In Spain it would be served with Ribeiro, the local wines of the region.

16 scallops
1 tablespoon lemon juice
1 medium onion
2 cloves garlic
2 hard-boiled eggs, shelled
50 g/2 oz fine fresh breadcrumbs
1 tablespoon chopped parsley
1½ teaspoons salt
pinch pepper
2 tablespoons olive oil

Open the scallops and remove the flesh. Discard all but the bright red coral and the white flesh, wash this thoroughly. Scrub the shells under cold running water until thoroughly clean, then set aside. Finely chop the scallop flesh and sprinkle with the lemon juice. Peel and chop the onion and garlic. Cut the eggs in half and remove the yolks. Set aside the yolks for use in another recipe, and finely chop the whites. Mix together the breadcrumbs, onion, garlic, egg whites, parsley and seasoning.

Heat the oil and stir into the breadcrumb mixture, then add the chopped scallops and mix thoroughly. Fill the scallop shells with the mixture and place in a moderately hot oven (190C, 375F, gas 5) for 10 to 15 minutes or until golden brown. Serve immediately as a first course.

Veal Escalopes with Orange Sauce

SERVES 4

4 veal escalopes, about 100 g/4 oz each
4 slices serrano *ham, or other lean smoked ham, about 225 g/8 oz*
1 teaspoon salt
¼ teaspoon pepper
1 egg, beaten
50 g/2 oz fine dried breadcrumbs
5 tablespoons olive oil
2 large potatoes
6 tablespoons milk
25 g/1 oz butter or margarine
pinch grated nutmeg

Sauce

1 small onion
2 teaspoons cornflour
150 ml/¼ pint fresh orange juice
grated rind of ½ orange
150 ml/¼ pint dry sherry

If the veal escalopes are too thick to roll up, flatten them with a meat mallet or rolling pin between two pieces of damp greaseproof paper. They should be the same size as the slices of ham. Place one slice of ham on each veal escalope and roll up with the veal on the outside. Secure with cocktail sticks, sprinkle with salt and pepper and coat with the beaten egg and then the breadcrumbs.

Heat the oil in a frying pan and sauté the veal rolls for 10 to 15 minutes or until tender and golden brown. Drain on kitchen paper, place in a heated serving dish and keep hot.

Peel the potatoes and cut into small pieces. Cook in lightly salted boiling water until just cooked. Drain well and mash very thoroughly with the milk, butter or margarine and nutmeg.

While the potatoes are cooking, prepare the sauce. Peel and finely chop the onion. Reheat the oil remaining in the frying pan and sauté the onion until lightly browned. Stir in the cornflour and cook for 1 minute. Add the orange juice, ½ teaspoon of the grated orange rind and sherry, a little at a time, stirring thoroughly after each addition. Bring to the boil, stirring constantly, and simmer very gently for 5 minutes. Pour the orange sauce over the veal and ham rolls, garnish with piped mashed potato and the remaining grated orange rind and serve immediately.

Stuffed Onions

SERVES 4

The onions of Valencia are of superb quality and uniform shape, which makes them ideal for this dish.

1 clove garlic
350 g/12 oz lean minced pork
1 teaspoon salt
¼ teaspoon pepper
pinch ground cinnamon
2 teaspoons finely chopped fresh parsley
1 egg
2 tablespoons milk
3 teaspoons lemon juice
8 large Spanish onions
75 g/3 oz fine fresh breadcrumbs
25 g/1 oz plain flour, plus a little extra for coating
150 ml/¼ pint olive oil
2 tablespoons dry white wine
150 ml/¼ pint water

Peel and finely chop the garlic. Place the pork in a bowl, add the garlic, salt, pepper, cinnamon, parsley, egg, milk and lemon juice, and mix thoroughly together. Set aside.

Peel the onions and cut a thin slice off the top of each one. Carefully scoop out the inside of each onion and reserve, leaving only the two outer layers completely intact. Fill the onion shells with the peppered meat mixture, press the breadcrumbs on top, then roll the onions in flour to coat well. Heat the oil in a heavy frying pan over a low heat and fry the stuffed onions gently for about 20 minutes or until golden, basting them frequently. Remove and drain on kitchen paper, then place them in a shallow casserole.

Finely chop the reserved onion and sauté in the oil remaining in the frying pan until lightly browned and soft. Stir in the flour and cook for about 30 seconds. Remove from the heat and gradually stir in the wine and water, mixing well after each addition. Bring to the boil over a moderate heat, stirring constantly, until the mixture thickens, then spoon over the stuffed onions. Bake in a moderate oven (160 C, 325 F, gas 3) for about 1 hour or until tender. Serve immediately.

Veal Escalopes with Orange Sauce

FRIED CHICKEN WITH VEGETABLES

SERVES 4

1 chicken (about 1·5 kg/3 lb)
3 teaspoons salt
¼ teaspoon pepper
4 young globe artichokes
225 g/8 oz asparagus
1 medium onion
1 large carrot
2 cloves garlic
2 hard-boiled eggs
150 ml/¼ pint olive oil
1 tablespoon chopped fresh parsley
5 tablespoons white wine
150 ml/¼ pint water
1 large potato
450 g/1 lb fresh peas

Cut the chicken into eight pieces and sprinkle with half the salt and the pepper. Rinse the artichokes in cold water. Cut off and discard the stems, remove and discard the coarse outer leaves. Cut off the points of the leaves with scissors about 2·5 cm/1 in from the top. Boil the artichokes in lightly salted water for 25 to 30 minutes or until tender. Drain and cool, then remove and discard the chokes from the middle of the artichokes. Remove and discard the woody fibrous base from each asparagus spear and lightly scrape any coarse skin from the lower half of the stalk. Cook in lightly salted water for about 20 minutes or until tender, then drain well. Peel and chop the onion, carrot and garlic. Peel the hard-boiled eggs and pound them to a paste in a mortar.

Heat three-quarters of the oil in a saucepan and sauté the chicken pieces until lightly browned, then remove from the pan and set aside in a hot place. Sauté the onion, carrot, garlic and parsley for about 5 minutes or until lightly browned. Return the fried chicken to the pan and add the wine, water and remaining salt. Bring to the boil, lower the heat and simmer for 8 minutes.

Meanwhile, peel the potato and cut into 1-cm/½-in cubes. Heat the remaining oil in a frying pan and sauté the potato cubes for 5 to 6 minutes or until cooked and golden brown. Drain on kitchen paper. Add the potato cubes to the saucepan along with the artichokes, asparagus, peas and the pounded eggs (which will thicken the sauce). Simmer for a further 15 to 20 minutes or until the chicken is tender. Serve immediately.

VALENCIAN PAELLA

SERVES 6

(Illustrated on front cover)

The Paella is the truly typical dish of Valencia and the most internationally known representative of Spanish cuisine. The people of Valencia zealously uphold the authenticity and ritual of this dish, which is certainly one of the country's gastronomic treasures.

1 large chicken, about 1·5 kg/3 lb, or same weight chicken pieces
3 teaspoons salt
1 kg/2 lb fresh peas, or 225 g/8 oz frozen peas
225 g/8 oz French beans, fresh or frozen
1 medium tomato
1 clove garlic
5 tablespoons olive oil
1 litre/1¾ pints water
1 teaspoon ground paprika
3 saffron strands
12 canned, drained cooked snails
450 g/1 lb long-grain rice
1 lemon, cut into wedges to garnish

Cut the chicken into about 15 pieces and sprinkle with salt. Shell the peas, if using fresh ones. Trim the beans and cut into 5-7.5-cm/2-3-in pieces. Drop the tomato into boiling water for 1 minute, remove then peel it. Peel and chop the garlic. Heat the oil in a paella pan if you have one, or in a large, heavy frying pan. Sauté the chicken pieces for 5 minutes, then add the garlic and tomato and sauté for 2 minutes. Add the peas and beans and sauté for another 2 minutes. Add the water and paprika and bring to the boil, then add the saffron strands and the snails. Lower the heat and simmer for 20 minutes. Add about a cupful of boiling water, or enough to replace what has evaporated, raise the heat until the water is boiling rapidly and then stir in the rice. Boil for 2 minutes, then lower the heat and simmer gently for about 12 to 15 minutes or until the rice is tender and dry. Remove from the heat, but leave on the hot stove for 5 minutes, then garnish with wedges of lemon and serve straight from the pan. Each diner squeezes the juice from the lemon wedges over the paella.

Note: Mussels in shells can be used instead of snails; cleaned squid, sliced into rings, can be added; crab meat or cleaned crab claws and, of course, cooked prawns can be included.

POTATO OMELETTE

SERVES 4

One of the dishes from Castilian kitchens noted for its simplicity is the potato omelette. It is served at table as a second course but it is also traditional to make it at picnics. It may be eaten hot or cold.

4 large potatoes
1 medium onion
6 tablespoons olive oil
6 eggs
1 teaspoon salt

Peel the potatoes and cut into 5-mm/¼-in slices. Peel and very finely chop the onion. Heat three-quarters of the oil in a frying pan and sauté the potatoes for 5 minutes. Add the onion and sauté for a further 10 to 15 minutes or until the potatoes and onion are soft but not brown, then remove them with a perforated spoon and allow to cool slightly on kitchen paper. Beat the eggs with the salt, add the potato and onion, and stir thoroughly.

Heat the remaining oil in a large omelette pan or heavy frying pan and add the egg mixture. When the omelette begins to set, lift the edge with a spatula and allow the unset egg to run underneath. When the omelette has a high, rounded edge, but is still soft in the centre, invert a lightly greased plate over the pan and turn the omelette on to it, then slide it back into the pan so the underside is now on top. Cook for 2 to 3 minutes, shaking the pan gently. Cut into portions and serve.

Variation

Diced green or red pepper, cooked peas or French beans, quartered button mushrooms, quartered, drained, canned artichoke hearts and roughly chopped peeled tomatoes can be added to the omelette. Chopped rindless bacon can be fried with the potatoes and onion if you like.

Mixed Vegetable Omelette

STUFFED TOMATOES

SERVES 6

This dish is served cold and may be eaten either as an hors d'oeuvre or as a salad. It is quite filling, so you will not need more than one large tomato (or two small ones) per person.

6 large or 12 medium tomatoes
2 heads lettuce
100 g/4 oz canned anchovy fillets
50 g/2 oz stoned green olives
1 medium onion
3 hard-boiled eggs
150 ml/¼ pint mayonnaise
½ teaspoon mustard
½ teaspoon lemon juice

Cut the tops off the tomatoes and discard, scoop out the seeds and flesh and reserve. Rinse the lettuce under cold running water, dry thoroughly, then shred finely and place on a large plate.

Drain and chop the anchovies and olives. Peel and finely chop the onion. Peel the hard-boiled eggs and separate the yolks from the whites. Finely chop three whites and two yolks, and sieve the remaining yolk. Mix together the tomato pulp, anchovies, olives, chopped egg, 1 tablespoon of the mayonnaise, mustard and lemon juice. Fill the tomatoes with this mixture and arrange them on the bed of shredded lettuce. Spoon the remaining mayonnaise over each tomato and garnish with the sieved egg yolk.

STUFFED PEPPERS

SERVES 4 or 8

Stuffed peppers are traditional dishes in many Spanish provinces, each district having its own variation. They are served at the table in the dish in which they were prepared and may be either a first or main course. If possible, this recipe should be made with red peppers, but if these are not available, the green ones may be used.

8 pigs' trotters, about 450-700 g/1-1½ lb each
8 red or green peppers
5 tablespoons olive oil
¼ teaspoon pepper
1 teaspoon salt
2 medium onions
2 cloves garlic
225 g/8 oz tomatoes
5 tablespoons dry white wine

Rinse the pigs' trotters thoroughly under cold running water, then place them in a large saucepan, add enough water to cover, and bring to the boil over a high heat. Lower the heat and simmer for about 1½ hours or until the meat comes away from the bones.

Arrange the peppers on a baking tray and place in a very hot oven (240C, 475F, gas 9) for 15 minutes or until the skins are split and charred. Remove from the oven and, when cool enough to handle, peel the peppers, cut off tops and keep, remove and discard the seeds. Place the peppers in a bowl, sprinkle with half the olive oil and the pepper and salt, and set aside for 1 hour.

Peel and chop the onions and garlic. Remove the seeds from the tomatoes and chop the flesh. Heat the remaining oil in a frying pan and sauté the onion and garlic until soft. Add the tomatoes and sauté until reduced to a pulp. Stir in the wine and set aside.

Drain the pigs' trotters and, when cool enough to handle, remove the meat from the bones and chop the meat finely. Mix with the onion mixture and spoon into the prepared pepper shells. Replace the tops and seal each opening with a cocktail stick, place the peppers in an ovenproof casserole, and brush with olive oil. Bake in a moderate oven (180C, 350F, gas 4) for about 30 minutes or until lightly browned. Serve hot with rice and a salad.

Spanish Doughnuts

SPANISH DOUGHNUTS

MAKES 30

The secret of these doughnuts is to fry them in plenty of oil so they can float freely and become rounded. They may be eaten hot or cold, at breakfast, with morning coffee, or as a dessert.

50 g/2 oz lard
½ teaspoon salt
6 tablespoons water
175 g/6 oz plain flour
6 eggs
oil for deep frying
50 g/2 oz caster sugar
150 ml/¼ pint double cream, whipped (optional)

Place the lard, salt and water in a small saucepan and bring to the boil over a moderate heat. Remove from the heat, add the flour and beat well, forming a smooth paste. Return the pan to the heat and cook for 2 minutes, beating constantly, until a smooth, stiff dough is formed. Remove from the heat and allow to cool for 2 minutes, then add the eggs, one at a time, beating well after each addition.

Heat the oil for deep-frying to 190 C/375 F, or until a cube of bread browns in 30 seconds. Drop generous teaspoons of the dough into the hot oil and fry for 3 to 4 minutes. The dough will rise to the top of the oil, and after about 2 minutes will automatically turn over. The doughnuts should be golden brown on the outside and slightly soft in the centre. Drain well on kitchen paper and sprinkle with sugar. Serve warm or cold.

If serving cold, make a cut along the side of each doughnut and fill with whipped cream. To do this, the cream can be put into a piping bag fitted with a large star nozzle or it can be spooned into the doughnuts.

Turkey

As in other Mediterranean countries, Turkish cooking is not a matter to be taken lightly; not a case of throwing a few ingredients into a pan just before the meal. Centuries of traditions make up a cuisine which is rich in the use of dairy produce, oil and spices. Vegetables, including okra, aubergines, artichokes and spinach, also form an important part of the diet in this agricultural country.

Fish, poultry and meat, rice and wheat are all cooked by various methods, often flavoured with herbs and pine-nut kernels. Pastries, both sweet and savoury, are popular and pastryshops are as much a feature of Turkish towns as coffee shops.

You will find a few examples of sweet dishes at the end of the chapter, including Turkish Delight. It is not very difficult to make and the home-made version is both delicately flavoured and fragrant – the perfect sweetmeat to offer at the end of a splendid meal.

So select a menu from the pages which follow and serve a feast of Turkish food for your family and friends to enjoy.

Stuffed Mackerel

SERVES 4

The flesh of the mackerel is somewhat oily since the fish belongs to the same family as the tuna. The mackerel used for this dish is traditionally about 450 g/1 lb in weight, so one fish per person should be enough.

4 large mackerel, about 450 g/1 lb each
Stuffing
4 small onions
6 tablespoons olive oil
2 tablespoons finely chopped fresh parsley
15 g/½ oz currants
4 teaspoons chopped fresh dill or 2 teaspoons dried dill
1 teaspoon ground cinnamon
salt and pepper
15 g/½ oz pine-nut kernels
6 tablespoons water
flour for coating
1 lemon, sliced to garnish

Remove the fins from the mackerel without breaking the skin. With a sharp knife or scissors, make a cut along the underside of the fish to within about 2·5 cm/1 in of the head and tail, and clean the fish. Snip the backbone at each end from the inside, and very gently ease out the bone, removing as little of the flesh as possible. To help loosen the backbone, lightly press along the bone on the outside of the fish, without breaking the skin. Wash the fish inside and out and dry with kitchen paper.

To make the stuffing, peel and finely chop the onions. Heat half the oil in a large frying pan, add the onions and sauté gently until soft. Add the parsley, currants, dill, cinnamon, salt and pepper and pine-nut kernels. Sauté for a further 5 to 10 minutes, stirring frequently until the mixture begins to brown. Add the water and simmer for 5 to 10 minutes until all the liquid has evaporated. Remove from the heat and allow to cool slightly, then spoon the stuffing into the cavities and loosely sew up the openings with thread, or insert several small skewers to close. Coat the fish with flour.

Heat the remaining oil in the frying pan over a very moderate heat and cook the fish for about 8 to 10 minutes on each side. Remove from the pan, drain on kitchen paper, and remove the thread or skewers. Serve the fish hot or cold, garnished with the lemon slices.

WHITEBAIT PILAFF

SERVES 4

A pilaff made with whitebait is a truly regional dish. Here, whitebait or sprats are cooked with rice and served hot like a kedgeree.

225 g/8 oz whitebait or sprats
50 g/2 oz butter
450 g/1 lb long-grain rice
salt and pepper
pinch ground cinnamon
600 ml/1 pint water

Wash the fish under cold running water and drain well. Heat the butter in a large saucepan and add the rice, stirring with a wooden spoon until the grains begin to turn white and opaque. Put the fish into the saucepan and mix well. Add seasoning to taste and the cinnamon. Add the water and bring to the boil quickly, then reduce the heat to very low, cover the pan tightly and simmer for 30 minutes without removing the lid. Turn the rice over with a thin spatula, cover the pan again and cook for a further 10 minutes. Serve hot.

FRIED RED MULLET

SERVES 4

Red mullet are at their best before they grow too large but they are also a great delicacy and are rather expensive when small.

8 red mullet, about 225 g/8 oz each
and not more than 23 cm/9 in long
50 g/2 oz plain flour
oil for shallow frying
few sprigs parsley
salt
2 lemons, cut into quarters

Descale and clean the red mullet, but do not remove the heads and tails. Wash the fish under cold running water, then dry with a cloth or kitchen paper. Coat each fish thoroughly with the flour, then shake them by the tail to remove any excess.

Heat the oil in a heavy frying pan and fry the fish for about 5 minutes on each side until golden brown. Drain on absorbent kitchen paper. Wash and dry the sprigs of parsley and sauté in the oil remaining in the pan until crisp. Drain well on absorbent kitchen paper. Arrange the red mullet on a heated serving dish, sprinkle with salt to taste and garnish with the parsley and lemon quarters. Serve immediately.

Fried Red Mullet

Note: To descale fish, hold it by the tail in a sink and use a kitchen knife to scrape off the scales, working down the body from the tail towards the head. The scales tend to flick off, which is why it is best to hold the fish in the sink.

STUFFED MUSSELS

SERVES 4

Select large mussels for this dish, since the smaller ones are more difficult to fill. Allow four to six mussels per serving.

16-24 mussels
1 large onion
1 tablespoon finely chopped fresh parsley
4 tablespoons olive oil
225 g/8 oz long-grain rice
3 tablespoons tomato purée
salt and pepper
600 ml/1 pint water
Garnish
1 tomato, cut into wedges
few sprigs parsley

Wash the mussels well under running water, scrubbing them to remove any seaweed and sand and remove the beards. Discard any mussels which are open and do not shut when tapped. Leave to soak for about an hour in plenty of cold water, and discard any that rise to the surface.

Peel and finely chop the onion and place in a large saucepan with the parsley and one-third of the oil. Add the mussels, cover the pan tightly, and cook over a high heat for 5 to 6 minutes, shaking the pan from time to time, until all the mussels have opened. Discard any that do not open. Remove the saucepan from the heat and set it aside to cool. Carefully remove the mussels from their shells without splitting the shells completely open, and reserve the shells.

Heat the remaining oil in a second saucepan, add the rice and cook over a high heat, stirring constantly, until the rice beomes opaque. Stir in the mussels, tomato purée, seasoning to taste and water. Bring to the boil, then reduce the heat and simmer, completely covered, for 30 minutes.

Remove the pan from the heat and set it aside to cool. Spoon the rice and mussel mixture into the reserved shells so that the rice is visible between the shells. Arrange the stuffed shells in a serving dish, then set aside to cool. Serve cold garnished with tomato wedges and parsley.

CHICK PEA AND CHICKEN CASSEROLE

SERVES 6

Traditionally, this dish was cooked and served in an earthenware pot, but it may also be cooked and served in a cast-iron casserole, or served in a tureen.

225 g/8 oz chick peas
salt and pepper
1 chicken, about 1·4 kg/3 lb or pieces to the same weight
225 g/8 oz shallots
50 g/2 oz butter
1 teaspoon chopped fresh parsley
¼ teaspoon dried thyme
½ teaspoon chopped fresh rosemary or ¼ teaspoon dried rosemary
pinch sugar

Soak the chick peas overnight in cold water, drain well, then place in a pan with plenty of salted water and bring to the boil. Reduce the heat, cover the pan and cook for about 40 minutes or until the chick peas are just tender. Drain and reserve. Cut the chicken into six portions. Peel the shallots and leave them whole.

Melt the butter in a flameproof casserole over a moderate heat and add the shallots and chicken. Sauté until the shallots just begin to soften. Add the drained chick peas, parsley, thyme, rosemary, sugar, seasoning to taste and just enough boiling water to cover the ingredients. Cover the casserole and cook in a moderately hot oven (200 C, 400 F, gas 6) for 50 to 60 minutes or until the pieces of chicken are cooked through. Check the water from time to time and add a little more if necessary. At the end of cooking most of the water should be absorbed, leaving a small amount of liquid. Serve hot.

Chicken with Boiled Rice

SERVES 6

This easily digestible dish was specially created for occasions where a light, but strengthening food was required. However, it is often cooked purely for its delicate taste and for its gastronomic appeal.

1 chicken, about 1·5 kg/3 lb
2-3 medium onions
2 large carrots
1 bay leaf
1·4 litres/2½ pints water
450 g/1 lb long-grain rice
salt and pepper

Wipe the chicken inside and out with a damp cloth or kitchen paper. Peel the onions and leave them whole. Peel the carrots and cut them into large pieces. Place the chicken, onions and carrots in a large saucepan, add the bay leaf and water and bring to the boil over a moderate heat. Reduce the heat, and simmer gently for about 1 hour or until the chicken is very tender. Remove the chicken from the saucepan and set it aside to cool. Strain the broth into a bowl, discard the vegetables, and return the broth to the saucepan.

When the chicken is cool enough to handle, remove and discard the skin, cut the flesh into small pieces, discarding the bones, and return the chicken to the strained broth. Add the rice and seasoning to taste, tightly cover the pan and simmer over a very low heat for 35 minutes or until all the liquid has been absorbed and the rice is tender. Serve hot in heated soup plates, with a green salad as an accompaniment.

Stuffed Mussels (opposite page)

The Lady's Thigh

SERVES 4

The texture of the dish should be very tender, as the name implies, though some insist that the excellent taste is the reason for the name.

50 g/2 oz short-grain rice
450 g/1 lb finely minced lean lamb
1 teaspoon finely chopped fresh parsley
salt and pepper
flour for coating
75 g/3 oz butter or margarine
2 teaspoons olive oil
2 eggs, beaten with 2 teaspoons cold water

Cook the rice in lightly salted boiling water for 10 minutes. Drain and cool. Place the rice, lamb, parsley and seasoning to taste in a bowl and knead and squeeze together to make a soft paste. Shape the mixture into flat ovals about 1 × 5 cm/½ × 2 in on a floured board, making sure that each one is completely coated with flour.

Melt the butter or margarine and oil in a frying pan over a low heat. Dip each meat oval into the beaten egg mixture and immediately place it in the hot fat. The egg should spread out around the ovals into thin tentacles that become crisp. Cook for about 5 minutes on each side or until dark brown. Drain on kitchen paper and serve hot with a vegetable and French fried or mashed potatoes.

Skewered Lamb Rolls

SERVES 4

This dish which is a cross between meatballs and kebabs, is widely served in countries to the south of Turkey. The bread makes the meat go further, so it is an economical dish, but delicious when well prepared.

Marinade
1 large onion
1 tablespoon olive oil
Meatballs
450 g/1 lb finely minced lamb
salt and pepper
1 slice stale white bread
sprigs of parsley or lettuce leaves

To make the marinade, peel and finely slice the onion and mix with the olive oil in a bowl.

Place the lamb and seasoning to taste in a bowl. Remove the crusts from the bread and soak the bread in a little cold water for 2 minutes, then squeeze out as much water as possible and add the bread to the meat. Knead the ingredients together to form a soft mixture. With damp hands, shape the meat mixture into cylindrical shapes about 7·5 cm/3 in long and 2·5 cm/1 in thick. Put the rolls into the marinade and let stand for at least 2 hours.

Place the meatballs lengthways on skewers and either barbecue or grill them for about 8 to 10 minutes, turning frequently until cooked on all sides. Serve hot on a bed of parsley sprigs or lettuce leaves, with rice and yogurt, if liked.

LAMB WITH OKRA

SERVES 4

This is really a type of *kapama* (smothered meat), but since the shape of the okra does not allow them to completely cover – or smother – the meat, the term is not applied to this dish.

675-900 g/1 ½-2 lb lean lamb, cut from the leg
2 large onions
450 g/1 lb okra
1 ½ tablespoons lemon juice
50 g/2 oz butter or margarine
1 teaspoon chopped fresh parsley
1 ½ teaspoons chopped fresh marjoram or 1 teaspoon dried marjoram
salt and pepper
250 ml/8 fl oz water

Cut the lamb into 7·5-cm/3-in pieces. Peel and thickly slice the onions. Wash the okra. Trim the stems, shaping the end into a cone and taking care not to cut through the flesh. Cover the okra with water and add the lemon juice to prevent discoloration. Rinse thoroughly and drain.

Melt the butter or margarine in a saucepan over a moderate heat, add the onions and sauté gently until soft but not browned. Add the pieces of lamb, increase the heat slightly, and sauté the lamb with the onions until the meat is lightly browned. Add the parsley, marjoram, seasoning to taste and the water. Tightly cover the pan and cook for 30 minutes. Add the okra, replace the lid, and cook for a further 20 minutes. Check the amount of liquid in the saucepan 10 minutes before the end of the cooking time. If there is a lot of liquid, remove the lid and allow some to evaporate. Place the meat and okra in a heated serving dish and serve hot.

Lamb with Okra

Lamb Wrapped in Aubergine

SERVES 4

This exceptionally tasty and fragrant dish is popular from Kabul in Afghanistan to the Middle East. The succulent melon-shaped variety of aubergine which grows in Bursa makes this dish a regional speciality, although any type of aubergine may be used.

675 g/1 ½ lb lamb, cut from the leg or shoulder
4 aubergines
salt
2 large onions
50 g/2 oz butter or margarine
pepper
1 teaspoon chopped fresh parsley
about 300 ml/½ pint water
6 tablespoons olive oil
1 large tomato

Cut the lamb into 7·5-cm/3-in pieces. Remove and discard the stems from the aubergines and slice the aubergines lengthways into the same number of slices as there are pieces of lamb. Sprinkle the slices very lightly with salt and set aside until required. Peel and coarsely chop the onions. Melt the butter or margarine in a saucepan over a moderate heat and sauté the onions until golden brown. Add the pieces of meat and sauté until browned, turning them frequently. Add seasoning to taste, the parsley and the water. Cover, and simmer for 35 to 40 minutes, then remove from the heat and let stand until cool.

Rinse the aubergine slices under cold running water and dry them thoroughly. Heat the oil in a frying pan over a moderate heat and sauté the slices until lightly browned on both sides. Drain well on kitchen paper. Wrap one slice of aubergine around each piece of lamb and place in a flameproof casserole. Pour over the liquid remaining in the saucepan.

Thinly slice the tomato, cut the slices in half, and top each wrapped piece of lamb with one half slice of tomato. Cover the casserole, place it over a moderate heat, and simmer for 30 to 40 minutes. Either serve hot from the casserole, or transfer to a heated serving dish, being careful to disturb the aubergine as little as possible, and pour over the sauce from the casserole.

Haricot Beans with Lamb

SERVES 4 to 6

In the preparation of this national dish, always use at least twice the amount of onions as beans.

225 g/8 oz dried haricot beans
225 g/8 oz lean lamb, cut from the leg
675 g/1 ½ lb onions
75 g/3 oz butter or margarine
salt and pepper
pinch sugar

Soak the beans overnight or for at least 2 hours in plenty of cold water. Drain the beans, put them in a saucepan and add enough fresh water to just cover them. Place over a high heat and bring to the boil, then lower the heat and continue cooking for 30 minutes, when they should be half cooked. Drain well.

Cut the lamb into 5-cm/2-in pieces. Peel and coarsely chop the onions. Melt the butter in a saucepan over a moderate heat, add the onions and sauté until soft and golden brown. Add the lamb and cook until browned. Add the beans, seasoning to taste, sugar and enough water to cover, and cook for 1 ½ hours. If the lamb is not tender after this time, add a little more warm water, replace the lid, and continue to simmer for a further 30 minutes, stirring occasionally. Place in a heated serving dish and serve hot, accompanied by White Pilaff (page 70).

Note: Canned beans can be substituted for dried beans. The drained beans should be added about 20 minutes before the lamb is cooked.

Lamb Wrapped in Aubergines

GREEN BEANS WITH LAMB

SERVES 4

In the Eastern Mediterranean there are several types of green beans suitable for this recipe. However, In Izmir, tender young French beans are the preferred choice.

1 kg/2 lb French beans, fresh or frozen or thawed
100 g/4 oz lamb, cut from the leg
1 medium onion
50 g/2 oz butter
2 tablespoons tomato purée
150 ml/¼ pint chicken stock
¼ teaspoon chopped fresh parsley
¼ teaspoon sugar
salt and pepper

Trim the beans if using fresh ones, then cut them into 5-7·5-cm/2-3-in pieces. Cut the lamb into 1-cm/½-in cubes. Peel and finely chop the onion.

Heat the butter in a saucepan over a moderate heat, add the onion and sauté until golden brown. Add the lamb and cook until brown, stirring occasionally. Stir in the tomato purée and immediately add the beans. Stir the mixture continuously until the beans darken in colour, then add the stock, parsley, sugar and seasoning to taste. Bring to the boil, then lower the heat and cover the pan. Cook gently for about 1 hour, or until the lamb is tender. Check to make sure the liquid does not evaporate, adding extra water if necessary. Pour into a heated serving dish and serve hot.

MEATBALLS WITH LEMON SAUCE

SERVES 6

This mixture of egg and lemon, also popular in Greek cuisine, is added to certain soups or poured over vegetables to enhance their quality and flavour. The lemon juice is believed to make the dish more digestible and refined, like an educated person, hence the dish's Turkish name *terbiye*, which means education.

Meatballs
675 g/1 ½ lb finely minced lean lamb or beef
salt and pepper
plain flour for coating
1 litre/1 ¾ pints beef stock
1 teaspoon finely chopped fresh parsley
Sauce
2 egg yolks
2 tablespoons lemon juice
stock

Season the lamb or beef well, and mix thoroughly with damp hands. Work the meat into a rope, about 1 cm/½ in thick. Break off small amounts and roll them into egg-shaped balls, about 1 cm/½ in. in diameter. Coat the meatballs with flour. Heat the beef stock to boiling in a saucepan over a high heat, then reduce the heat and drop in the meatballs a few at a time. Simmer very gently for about 10 minutes or until the meatballs rise to the surface. Add the parsley and remove the pan from the heat.

To make the sauce, beat the egg yolks and lemon juice in a small bowl. Stirring constantly, gradually add 6 tablespoons of hot stock taken from the saucepan in which the meatballs were cooked. Pour the egg-yolk mixture back into the hot stock, stirring constantly, and reheat the stock to simmering point, if necessary, but do not reboil. Transfer the meatballs with the sauce to a heated serving dish and serve immediately.

LAMB'S LIVER PILAFF

SERVES 4

This may be used as a stuffing for lamb, or it can be served as an accompaniment either to roast lamb or lamb cooked on the spit.

100 g/4 oz lamb's liver
50 g/2 oz butter or margarine
1 teaspoon pine-nut kernels
1 teaspoon currants
1 tablespoon chopped fresh dill or 2 teaspoons dried dill
1 tablespoon chopped fresh parsley
½ teaspoon ground cinnamon
salt and pepper
225 g/8 oz long-grain rice
about 500 ml/17 fl oz water

Wash the liver and cut it into 5-mm/¼-in cubes. Melt the butter or margarine in a medium-sized saucepan over a moderate heat and sauté the liver until it just begins to brown. Add the pine-nut kernels and continue cooking, stirring frequently, for 4 to 5 minutes. Add the currants, dill, parsley, cinnamon, seasoning to taste and the rice. When the rice becomes opaque, remove the saucepan from the heat and gradually stir in the water. After each addition, push a spoon across the bottom of the saucepan from the near side toward the opposite side. When enough water has been added, the rice will form a peak just above the surface of the liquid, about three-quarters of the way across the saucepan.

Place the saucepan over a high heat and bring to the boil. Lower the heat, tightly cover the pan, and cook the rice for 25 minutes, then remove the lid and stir the rice into a cone in the centre. Replace the lid and leave the saucepan on a low heat for a further 5 minutes, then remove from the heat, take off the lid, and let the rice stand for 3 minutes. Heap the rice into a cone shape on a heated plate and serve hot.

Lamb's Liver Pilaff

Pastries Stuffed with Cottage Cheese

SERVES 4 to 6

Stuffed pastries, known as *börekler* are a well known Middle Eastern delicacy. The fillings may be varied to include minced meat with onions, spinach or courgettes.

175 g/6 oz cottage or curd cheese
2 teaspoons finely chopped fresh parsley
2 teaspoons finely chopped fresh mint
salt and pepper
100 g/4 oz puff pastry, thawed if frozen
1 egg, beaten with 1 teaspoon cold water
few sprigs parsley

Set the oven to moderately hot (190 C, 375 F, gas 5) and lightly grease a baking tray. Mix together the cottage cheese, parsley, mint and seasoning to taste. Roll out the pastry on a well-floured surface to about 3 mm/⅛ in thick, then cut it into 16 5-7·5-cm/2-3-in squares. Place an equal amount of the cottage cheese filling on each square, dampen the edges of the pastry and fold the squares into triangles, pressing the edges firmly together. Place the pastries on a baking tray about 1 cm/½ in apart, and brush with the beaten egg.

Bake in the pre-heated oven for 25 to 30 minutes or until crisp and golden brown.

Separate the pastries with a spatula or knife and arrange them on a heated serving plate. Garnish with sprigs of parsley and serve while still hot. Yogurt may be served separately.

Variation

Proceed as above, but instead of cutting the pastry into small squares, cut into two equal-sized pieces. Place half on a well-greased baking tray, and place spoonsful of the cottage cheese mixture about 3·5 cm/1½ in apart on the pastry. Brush the spaces between the filling with beaten egg or water. Place the remaining half of the pastry over the filling and firmly press together the layers of pastry between the filling and around the edge.

Brush with beaten egg and bake as above, then cut into diamond shapes and serve while still hot, garnished with sprigs of parsley.

Courgettes with Chick Peas

SERVES 4

The chick peas in this delicate and finely flavoured dish are used primarily for decoration and the absorption of excess juices.

25 g/1 oz chick peas
6 large or 8 small courgettes
75 g/3 oz butter or margarine
1 medium onion
1 chicken wing
salt and pepper
2 tablespoons chopped fresh parsley
3 tablespoons chicken stock

Soak the chick peas overnight in cold water. Drain before using, and discard any particles of husk which float to the surface. Rinse the courgettes under cold running water, then cut them into 1-cm/½-in slices.

Melt the butter or margarine in a small saucepan over a low heat, add the courgettes and tightly cover the pan. Shake the saucepan over the heat, holding the lid in place, so that the courgettes are coated in the butter, and sauté very gently for 5 minutes. Remove the pan from the heat and drain the excess butter into a medium-sized flameproof casserole. Peel and finely chop the onion and place in the bottom of the casserole with the chicken wing in the centre. Carefully spoon the chick peas over and around the chicken wing, and place the courgettes in layers around the outer edge of the casserole, adding a sprinkling of salt, pepper and parsley between each layer. When the courgettes are level with the chick peas, continue to layer the courgettes towards the chicken wing in the centre. Add the stock, cover the casserole with a small plate and then with the lid. Place over a low heat and cook for 1 hour. Serve direct from the casserole.

WINTER VEGETABLE CASSEROLE

SERVES 6

This recipe is a Kiş (winter) dish, using winter vegetables, though cabbage and cauliflower are thought to be too strong in aroma to use in this case. Cubes of lamb may also be added for a meat-based casserole.

1 celeriac
3-6 medium carrots
3 medium leeks
2 medium turnips
1-2 medium onions
50 g/2 oz butter or margarine
pinch dried thyme
pinch dried rosemary
salt and pepper
meat stock or water

Peel the celeriac and cut it into 2·5-3·5-cm/1-1½-in cubes. Peel and cut the carrots into slices. Trim, thoroughly wash and slice the leeks. Peel the turnips and potatoes and cut them into 2·5-3·5-cm/1-1½-in cubes. Peel and coarsely chop the onions.

Melt the butter or margarine in a saucepan over a moderate heat. Add the onions and sauté until transparent and beginning to brown. Add the celeriac, carrots, leeks, turnips, potatoes, thyme, rosemary and seasoning to taste, and cook for 3 to 4 minutes, stirring frequently. Add enough stock or water to partially cover the vegetables. Tightly cover the saucepan and simmer for 40 to 45 minutes or until tender. Remove from the heat, transfer the vegetables to a heated serving dish and serve hot.

Winter Vegetable Casserole

Artichokes in Olive Oil

ARTICHOKES IN OLIVE OIL

SERVES 4

This is a sophisticated dish, and the dome-like artichokes standing erect in the dish with the stems trimmed to resemble minarets, are a visual delight. Great care should be taken to choose artichokes which, although fully grown, are still young enough to be tender. Their stems should be about 5 cm/2 in long.

4 globe artichokes · 1 lemon
2 large potatoes
100 g/4 oz shallots
3 tablespoons olive oil
225 g/8 oz fresh or frozen broad beans (weight without pods)
salt and pepper
1 tablespoon chopped fresh dill or 2 teaspoons dried dill
½ teaspoon chopped fresh parsley
few sprigs parsley to garnish

Peel off and discard the coarse outer leaves of the artichokes until you reach the soft, blue-tinted inner leaves. Cut the artichokes horizontally with a sharp knife and remove the soft leaves and the choke (the hairy core in the centre), leaving a half-sphere with the stem as a handle. Trim the stem of each artichoke until it is flat-sided and about 5 mm/¼ in square. Cut the lemon in half. Rub the artichokes with one half of the lemon and squeeze the juice from the remaining half into a bowl of water. Add the prepared artichokes and leave to soak until required. Peel the potatoes, and cut them into quarters lengthways. Peel the shallots and leave them whole.

Heat the olive oil in a saucepan over a moderate heat. Add the shallots and sauté until almost soft, but not browned. Add the beans, seasoning to taste, dill, chopped parsley and enough water to just cover the vegetables, and simmer very gently for about 5 minutes or until the shallots are fully cooked. Drain the artichokes, add them to the saucepan, and simmer for 20 minutes, adding more water if necessary. Add the potatoes and simmer for a further 20 minutes or until all the vegetables are tender. Remove the saucepan from the heat and leave to cool.

Stand the artichokes, stems upwards, on a china dish. Spoon the other vegetables and the juice around them, garnish with the parsley sprigs and serve cold.

BUTTERED SPINACH WITH YOGURT

SERVES 4

Spinach cooked this way is delicious, especially when served with yogurt. It can also be used as a filling for an omelette or as an accompaniment for poached eggs or grilled cutlets.

900 g/2 lb fresh spinach
1 large onion
50 g/2 oz butter
salt and pepper
Sauce
450 ml/¾ pint natural yogurt
salt and pepper

Wash the spinach thoroughly under cold running water. Remove and discard the thick stems, tear the spinach into shreds and drain in a colander. Peel and finely chop the onion.

Melt the butter in a saucepan over a moderate heat. Add the onion and sauté until transparent but not browned, stirring occasionally. Add the spinach, a little at a time, stirring constantly, until all has been added. There is no need to add water because the spinach will produce plenty of liquid. Season to taste and cook gently until all the liquid has evaporated and the spinach is dark green. Place the spinach in a serving dish and make a well in the centre. Beat the yogurt with a little salt and pepper to taste, and pour into the well in the spinach. Serve immediately.

CABBAGE PURÉE

SERVES 4

The delicate flavour of nutmeg makes this dish a particularly suitable accompaniment to any fried, grilled or roast meat – especially in the winter. White cabbage is best suited for this dish as it does not retain as much liquid as green, but even so, it is important to squeeze out as much of the water as possible. The purpose of the added flour is to absorb any surplus.

1 white cabbage, about 1·4 kg/3 lb
1 teaspoon salt
25 g/1 oz plain flour
300 ml/½ pint milk
½ teaspoon grated nutmeg
salt and pepper

Remove and discard the coarse outer leaves from the cabbage, cut it in half lengthways and remove and discard the hard centre core. Separate the leaves and cut out the thick part of each rib. Place the cabbage in a saucepan, add water to cover and the salt, and simmer for 10 to 15 minutes or until tender. Drain well in a wire sieve or colander, then press a plate or saucer on top to squeeze out the excess water. Chop the cabbage very finely with a sharp knife or shred in a food processor.

Placed the chopped cabbage in a heavy saucepan over a low heat. Blend the flour to a smooth, soft paste with a little of the milk. Stir the flour paste into the cabbage and slowly add the remaining milk, stirring constantly until the mixture thickens. Simmer for 15 minutes. Add the nutmeg and seasoning to taste, and simmer for a further 5 minutes. Pour into a heated serving dish and serve hot.

Sour Leeks

SOUR LEEKS

SERVES 4

Traditionally, only the white part of the leeks are used in this recipe, which is why so many leeks are needed. The green part may be used for another dish, or for soup or stock.

12 large leeks
3 tablespoons olive oil
1 tablespoon vinegar
1 teaspoon sugar
salt and pepper
1 tablespoon chopped fresh parsley

Cut off and discard the coarse green upper part of the leeks and trim off the roots. Cut off the tender green leaves and reserve them for another dish. Cut the white part of the leeks in half lengthways and rinse very thoroughly under cold running water to remove any dirt. Using a sharp knife, slice the leeks lengthways very finely.

Heat the oil in a heavy saucepan over a high heat, add the sliced leeks, and sauté until golden brown, stirring continuously. Lower the heat, add just enough water to cover the leeks, and stir in the vinegar, sugar and seasoning to taste. Simmer over a fairly low heat for 30 minutes, them remove from the heat, transfer to a serving dish, and set aside until cold. Serve sprinkled with the parsley. The leeks can be served as a vegetable dish or as a starter.

WHITE PILAFF

SERVES 6

Pilaffs are the traditional rice dish in the Eastern Mediterranean, and there are many varieties. The following recipe is the basic pilaff; variations may be made by adding additional ingredients or substituting chicken or meat stock for the water.

100 g/4 oz butter
450 g/1 lb long-grain rice
500 ml-1 litre/1½-2 pints water
salt and pepper

Heat the butter in a large, heavy saucepan. Stir in the rice and cook gently until most of the grains become opaque. Remove the saucepan from the heat and gradually stir in the water. After each addition, push the spoon across the bottom of the saucepan from the near side towards the opposite side. When enough water has been added, the rice will form a peak just above the surface of the liquid, about three-quarters of the way across the saucepan. Add seasoning to taste. Place the saucepan over a high heat and bring to the boil. Lower the heat, tightly cover the pan and cook for 25 minutes. Remove the lid and stir the rice gently with a wooden spoon, starting from the edges and heaping the rice into a cone in the centre. Replace the lid and leave the saucepan over a low heat for a further 5 minutes. Remove the pan from the heat, take off the lid and let the rice stand for 3 minutes. Use an as accompaniment or serve by itself, on a heated plate, heaped into a cone shape. If the pilaff is served on its own, a bowl of yogurt should accompany it, and the yogurt may be spooned over the rice.

Variations

Red pilaff: This variation is usually eaten unaccompanied or occasionally with meat. It is never mixed with other ingredients or served with yogurt. Proceed in the same way, but before adding the water, add 3 tablespoons tomato purée, then the water and continue as above.

Pilaff with thyme: Proceed as above, but before adding the water, add 2 teaspoons chopped fresh thyme or 1 teaspoon dried thyme. Add the water and continue as above.

THE IMAM FAINTED

SERVES 4

An Imam is a Moslem religious dignitary, and this legend concerns a famous Imam who was particularly fond of aubergine. One day, his wife prepared this version of his favourite vegetable – a dish so rich that the Imam swooned away.

4 aubergines
6 tablespoons olive oil
6 large onions
2 tablespoons pine-nut kernels
2 tablespoons currants
½ teaspoon ground cinnamon
½ teaspoon dried dill
½ teaspoon chopped fresh parsley
salt and pepper
1 medium tomato
Garnish
1 lemon, cut into wedges
few sprigs fresh parsley

Trim the stalks off the aubergines. Peel narrow strips of skin lengthways off the aubergines to give a striped effect (as shown in the picture). Lay the aubergines on their sides and cut a long oval wedge out of each one. Peel and chop these wedges.

Heat half the oil in a large frying pan over a moderate heat, and sauté the chopped aubergine until soft. Remove them from the pan and reserve. Peel and thinly slice the onions. Heat the remaining oil in the pan and sauté the onions until soft and transparent, but not browned. Replace the chopped aubergine, pine-nut kernels, currants, cinnamon, dill, parsley and seasoning to taste, mix thoroughly and sauté for 5 minutes, stirring frequently. Remove from the heat and cool.

Lay the uncooked aubergines with cut sides upwards, side by side in a large frying pan or saucepan with a lid. Pile the sautéed mixture into the wedge cuts and over the aubergines, then add enough water to come halfway up the sides of them. Drop the tomato into boiling water, then peel it, scoop out and discard the seeds, and cut the flesh into four small diamond-shaped pieces. Top the aubergines with the tomato. Cover the pan, place it over a moderate heat, and bring the liquid to the boil, then reduce the heat and simmer very gently for 40 to 50 minutes, or until tender.

Transfer to a serving dish and cool completely. Serve garnished with the lemon and parsley.

Cracked Wheat Pilaff

SERVES 6

In Istanbul, very near the stock exchange, there are small restaurants where this dish is prepared to perfection. It is very hot, although succulent, in the true Ayntep fashion. The pepper is toned down in this recipe, but this does not affect the marvellous taste.

225 g/8 oz cracked wheat (bulghur wheat)
225 g/8 oz lean lamb, cut from the leg
1 large onion
50 g/2 oz butter
salt and pepper
1 red chilli pepper pod (see note)

Wash the wheat in a sieve under cold running water, then soak in cold water for 1 hour. Cut the lamb into 2·5-cm/1-in cubes. Peel and finely chop the onion. Melt the butter in a saucepan over a moderate heat and sauté the onion until golden brown. Add the lamb and cook until it begins to brown. Add seasoning to taste and just enough water to cover the meat. Tightly cover the saucepan and boil the meat rapidly for 15 minutes, then reduce the heat to a minimum and simmer for a further 30 to 35 minutes or until all the liquid has been absorbed.

Drain the wheat and add it to the meat with the red pepper pod. Cook very slowly, adding warm water at frequent intervals, until the wheat has absorbed all the liquid. This will take 20 to 30 minutes. Heap the pilaff in a mound on a heated serving dish and place the red pepper pod on top. Serve without accompaniment, as a first course.

Note: The Italian type of long, red pepper pod less hot than chilli but more aromatic, is largely used in this region, but if these are not available, dried red chilli may be substituted.

Cracked Wheat Pilaff

Cucumber in Yogurt

SERVES 4

This peasant dish has been adopted by Istanbul and has become a classic. In Greece it is called *tzatziki*. It makes a most refreshing summer lunch with a bowl of olives and pitta bread or brown bread.

½ large cucumber
1 teaspoon finely chopped fresh mint
600 ml/1 pint natural yogurt
salt and pepper
olive oil (optional)

Peel and finely chop the cucumber, place it in a bowl, and add half the mint. Beat the yogurt with the seasoning to taste and mix into the cucumber. Adjust the seasoning if necessary. A little olive oil may be trickled over the surface if liked. Sprinkle with the remaining mint and serve well chilled.

Onion Salad

SERVES 4

3-4 large Spanish onions
4 tablespoons salt
1 teaspoon tarragon vinegar or other vinegar
4½ teaspoons lemon juice
1½ teaspoons cold water
salt and pepper
3 tablespoons olive oil
1 tablespoon coarsely chopped fresh parsley

Peel the onions and cut them in half. Place the cut sides down on a chopping board, and slice the onions lengthways very thinly. Place the sliced onions in a large wire sieve, sprinkle with the salt and press the onions and salt together until all the salt has dissolved. Rinse the onions thoroughly under cold running water and drain well.

Mix together the vinegar, lemon juice and water in a salad bowl and season with salt and pepper to taste. Beat in the olive oil gradually. Add the onion and parsley and mix thoroughly before serving.

Vizier's Fingers

SERVES 4

This semolina dessert was probably invented long ago at the palace of one of the Grand Viziers. It is a delicious dish with a wholesome buttery flavour.

100 g/4 oz fine semolina
300 ml/½ pint milk
1 egg, beaten
100 g/4 oz caster sugar
300 ml/½ pint water
1½ tablespoons lemon juice
few drops almond essence
50 g/2 oz butter
few drops rose water (optional)

Place the semolina in a saucepan, stir in the milk and bring to the boil over a moderate heat, stirring constantly, until the mixture becomes very stiff. Remove from the heat and beat in the egg. Turn out on to a buttered plate or foil and let stand until cool.

Meanwhile, put the sugar, water and lemon juice into a heavy saucepan and stir over a low heat until the sugar dissolves. Add the almond essence and bring to the boil. Continue boiling until a thick syrup is formed, and as soon as it begins to turn golden brown, remove it from the heat, and set aside in a warm place.

Shape the cooled semolina mixture into finger shapes about 6 cm/2½ in long. Melt the butter in a heavy frying pan and sauté the fingers until browned on both sides. Remove them from the pan and drain them on kitchen paper. Arrange on a serving dish and pour over the warm syrup. Sprinkle with a few drops of rosewater just before pouring on the syrup, if liked. Serve cold.

Vizier's Fingers

Pumpkin Dessert

SERVES 4

There are two varieties of pumpkins most often used in Turkey for this dish. One is red, and the other a much larger green pumpkin, known as *cherkess* pumpkin.

about 450 g/1 lb fresh pumpkin
1 tablespoon water
25 g/1 oz caster sugar
1½ tablespoons lemon juice
100 g/4 oz finely chopped walnuts

Remove the seeds and the soft stringy pulp from the pumpkin flesh, but leave the pumpkin unpeeled. Cut it into four pieces, each about 5 × 7·5 cm/2 × 3 in, and place the pieces skin side upward in a saucepan. Add the water, tightly cover the pan, and cook very gently until the pumpkin is tender. Drain off the juice that forms during cooking into a measuring cup, and add water to make 300 ml/½ pint. Add the sugar and lemon juice and pour into a small saucepan. Heat gently to dissolve the sugar, then increase the heat and boil rapidly until reduced to about half.

Place the pumpkin in a serving dish with the skin side underneath, pour over the syrup, and sprinkle with the chopped walnuts. Serve warm or cold.

TURKISH DELIGHT

MAKES 1½ lb

Turkish delight is considered the epitomy of luxury in Eastern Mediterranean countries. In the old days, even the smallest café offered a piece of *lokum* with each cup of coffee ordered.

175 ml/6 fl oz water
3 tablespoons orange juice
3 tablespoons lemon juice
grated rind of 1 orange
grated rind of 1 lemon
675 g/1½ lb caster sugar
25 g/1 oz gelatine
75 g/3 oz cornflour
3-4 drops colouring (optional)
icing sugar for coating

Put the water, orange and lemon juice and rind and sugar into a heavy saucepan and bring to the boil over a low heat, taking care that the sugar has dissolved before boiling point is reached. Lower the heat and boil the liquid very gently until it reaches a temperature of 110 C/230 F and forms a long thread when lifted. Meanwhile, dissolve the gelatine in a little hot water.

Turkish Delight

Blend the cornflour with enough cold water to make a thin paste and add this to the hot syrup, stirring constantly. Boil the mixture until thick, stirring occasionally. Stir in the gelatine, off the heat, then add the colouring, if used. Pour the mixture into a 20-cm/8-in square cake tin. Set it aside for at least 24 hours.

Loosen the Turkish delight in the tin and turn it out on to a thick layer of icing sugar. Sprinkle the top with icing sugar and cut it into 2·5-cm/1-in squares with a sharp knife. Coat each square with icing sugar immediately.

Note: If desired, rosewater may be substituted for the orange and lemon juice.

Index